Edexcel GCSE
Maths

Achieve Grade 7–9 Workbook

Su Nicholson
Russell Timmins
Greg Byrd

Collins

William Collins' dream of knowledge for all began with the publication of his first book in 1819. A self-educated mill worker, he not only enriched millions of lives, but also founded a flourishing publishing house. Today, staying true to this spirit, Collins books are packed with inspiration, innovation and practical expertise. They place you at the centre of a world of possibility and give you exactly what you need to explore it.

Collins. Freedom to teach.

Published by Collins
An imprint of HarperCollins*Publishers*
The News Building
1 London Bridge Street
London
SE1 9GF

Browse the complete Collins catalogue at
www.collins.co.uk

10 9 8 7 6 5 4 3 2

ISBN 978-0-00-827125-1

British Library Cataloguing in Publication Data
A catalogue record for this publication is available from the British Library.

Authors: Su Nicholson, Russell Timmins, Greg Byrd
Commissioning editor: Rachael Harrison
In-house project editor: Isabelle Sinclair
Development editor: Joanne Crosby
Copyeditor: David Hemsley
Proofreader: Julie Bond
Answer checker: Deborah Dobson
Cover designer: The Big Mountain Design
Cover photos: © tj-rabbit/Shutterstock.com; chaoss/Shutterstock.com
Production controller: Tina Paul
Printed and bound by Martins the Printers

The publishers will gladly receive any information enabling them to rectify any error or omission at the first opportunity.

MIX
Paper from
responsible sources
FSC www.fsc.org **FSC™ C007454**

This book is produced from independently certified FSC paper to ensure responsible forest management.

For more information visit:
www.harpercollins.co.uk/green

Contents

Introduction

This workbook aims to help you reach your full potential and get an A* in your Mathematics GCSE. It gives you plenty of practice with brand new content in the key topics and main sections of your course.

These sections are colour coded: Number, Algebra, Geometry and Measures, Statistics and Probability.

Question grades

You can tell the grade of each question or question part by the colour of its number:

Grade 6 questions are show as **1**

Grade 7 questions are shown as **1**

Grade 8 questions are shown as **1**

Grade 9 questions are shown as **1**

Some Grade 6 questions have been included as a reminder of the pre-requisite prior knowledge for the higher-grade questions.

> Hint: Keep thinking – square numbers.

Hint boxes

The 'Hint' boxes provide you with guidance as to how to approach challenging questions.

Target questions

Grade 9 questions are marked with ◎ as a useful reminder of the top grade you are aiming for. These questions are the most difficult you will face and they are good practice to prepare for the top grade questions in your exam.

Problem solving

This section gives examples of problem solving questions. It helps to build your problem solving and communication skills.

Spot the errors

This part of the book promotes analytical thinking and problem solving. In each question there are one or more errors in student working. You need to look at the incorrect responses in the blue and yellow boxes marked with , show where the students went wrong and then work out the correct answer yourself.

Answers

You will find answers to all the questions at the back of the book. If you are working on your own you can check your answers yourself. If you are working in class your teacher may want to go through the answers with you.

How to interpret the language of exam questions

This section provides a helpful table that explains the wording used in exam questions and how to interpret it correctly to get full marks.

Formulae and helpful hints

Finally, you are provided with a list of formulae that you need to know and a list of the formulae which are given in the examination.

1 Number

1.1 Estimating powers and roots

Hint: In question 1(f), write 0.126 as 126×10^{-3}.

1 Use powers and roots that you know to estimate the value of each of the following.

a $3.1^4 = $ _____

b $\sqrt{63.8} = $ _____

c $(0.49)^3 = $ _____

d $82^{\frac{1}{4}} = $ _____

e $\sqrt[3]{26.85} = $ _____

f $(0.126)^{\frac{2}{3}} = $ _____

Hint: In questions 2 and 3, use a number line to help.

2 Estimate the following to 1 decimal place.

a $\sqrt{34.5} = $ _____

b $\sqrt{219.8} = $ _____

c $\sqrt{1.36} = $ _____

3 Estimate the following to the nearest whole number.

a $(5.6)^2 = $ _____

b $(12.3)^2 = $ _____

c $(14.8)^2 = $ _____

4 Estimate the value of the following. Show your working.

Hint: A realistic mental estimate of $17.5 \times \sqrt{39}$ is $20 \times 6 = 120$.

a $18.7 \times \sqrt{10.01 - 0.45}$ _____

b $\sqrt{\dfrac{31.74^2}{8.75 + 6.61}}$ _____

c $\sqrt{0.23} \times \sqrt{0.17}$ _____

d $\dfrac{10 - \sqrt{9.09}}{\sqrt{0.26}}$ _____

e $\sqrt{\dfrac{3\sqrt{15.8} - 2.1^3}{(6.1)^4}}$ _____

1.2 Combinations and factors 🖩

Hint: If there are p ways of doing one task and q ways of doing a second task, then the total number of ways of doing the first task followed by the second task is $p \times q$.

1   An ice cream shop has 15 flavours of ice cream.

Petra wants one scoop of each of three different flavours.

Show that there are 2730 different ways of choosing the three scoops of ice cream.

> Hint: There are 15 ways to choose the first scoop, so how many ways are there to choose the second and then the third if the three scoops are all different?

_____

_____

2   A group of students go on a school exchange visit with their teacher.

There are 12 girls and 15 boys in the group.

a The teacher wants one girl and one boy from the group to attend a presentation.

Work out the number of different ways one girl and one boy can be chosen from the group.

_____

_____

b The teacher decides to take three students from the group to meet the local mayor.

Work out the number of different ways three students can be chosen from the group.

_____

_____

3   A menu has three types of topping for pizza: meat, vegetable and cheese. There are:

- six different meats
- five different vegetables
- three different cheeses.

Customers can choose the following combinations of toppings:

- one meat, one vegetable and one cheese
- one meat and one cheese
- one meat and one vegetable
- one vegetable and one cheese.

a Sophie wants a pizza with one vegetable topping and one cheese topping.

Work out the number of different pizzas she can choose from.

_____

_____

b Carlos wants a pizza with one meat topping, one vegetable topping and one cheese topping.

Work out the number of different pizzas he can choose from.

_____

_____

c Show that there are 63 different ways of choosing a pizza with two types of topping from the menu.

_____

_____

4   **a**   Write 28, 105 and 350 as products of their prime factors.

     b   Use a Venn diagram to work out the HCF and LCM of the following.

        i   28 and 105 _____

        ii   28 and 350 _____

        iii   105 and 350 _____

        iv   28, 105 and 350 _____

5   In a group of 150 students, 72 study English, 70 study Maths, and 52 study Biology. 22 study English and Biology, 20 study Maths and English only, and 7 do not study any of these subjects.

Given that twice as many students study Maths and Biology only as study all three subjects:

a   Draw a Venn diagram to show this information.

b   Work out the number of students who study all three subjects.

_____

_____

1.3 Reverse percentages 🖩

> **Hint:** If an item decreases in value by 10% it is worth 90% of its original value. To find the value after a decrease of 10% you can multiply by 0.9 to find the new value in one step. 0.9 is called the 'multiplier'. To find the original value you reverse the process.

1 A Formula One racing car tyre loses approximately 10% of its weight during a race, due to wear. After a race a complete set of tyres weighs about 18 kg. What does the set weigh before the race?

_____

_____

2 In 2018, after a 150% increase in salary, a Formula One driver was estimated to earn around $18 million. How much did he earn in 2017?

_____

_____

3 If, three years ago, a Formula One driver had put that year's earnings into a bank account at 5% compound interest, he would now have $7 938 000 in his account. How much did he earn three years ago?

_____

_____

4 A new Lexus car lost 33% of its value in year 1 and 19% of its value in year 2. At the end of year 2 the value of the car was £36 825. What was the value of the car when new?

_____

_____

5 Brad invested some money in shares. In the first year the value of the shares increased by 2.9%. In the second year the value increased by 3.15%.

What is the overall percentage change in the value of the shares?

_____

_____

6 Kerry bought a flat. The value of her flat went down by 2% in the first year. In the second year the value went up by 5%. At the end of the second year, her house was worth £265 700.

a What is the percentage change in the value of the house? _____

_____

b Work out how much Kerry paid for her flat.

_____

_____

1.4 Standard form 🖩

Hint: A number is in standard form when it is in the form $a \times 10^n$, where $1 \leqslant a < 10$ and n is an integer.

1 An average person has approximately 2×10^{13} red corpuscles in their bloodstream. Each red corpuscle weighs about 0.000 000 000 1 grams. Work out the approximate total mass of the red corpuscles in an average person, in kilograms.

_____

_____

2 A factory produces nails. Each nail has a mass of 5×10^{-3} kg.

0.75% of the nails produced by the factory are faulty.

a The factory produces 3.6×10^{6} nails in one year.

Work out the total mass of the faulty nails produced in one year.

_____

b The mass of the faulty nails in one batch produced by the factory was 4.5×10^{-1} kg.

   i Work out the total mass of the nails in the batch. Give your answer in standard form.

_____

   ii How many nails were in the batch?

_____

3 The speed of light is 3×10^{8} metres per second.

a The distance between the Earth and the Sun is 1.5×10^{8} kilometres.

How many seconds does it take for light to travel from the Sun to the Earth?

_____

b Light takes 1 hour 25 minutes to travel from the Sun to Saturn. How far is the Sun from Saturn, in kilometres? Give your answer in standard form.

_____

4 The surface area of Earth is 510 072 000 km².

The surface area of Saturn is 42.7 billion km².

How many times greater is the surface area of Saturn than the surface area of Earth?

Give your answer in standard form.

_____

5 $p^2 = \dfrac{a - b}{ab}$

$a = 6.2 \times 10^8$

$b = 4.5 \times 10^7$

Find the value of p.

Give your answer in standard form correct to 2 significant figures.

_____

6 There are approximately 15 500 bacterium cells per square centimetre of skin on the human body.

An average human body has 2 square metres of skin.

The mass of one bacterium is 9.5×10^{-13} g.

What is the total weight in grams of the bacteria on an average human body?

Give your answer in standard form.

_____

_____

_____

1.5 Bounds

> **Hint:** The bounds of a measure are the highest and lowest possible values of the measure according to the limits of accuracy provided, e.g. the bounds of a weight, w kg, which is 1.3 kg rounded to 1 decimal place are $1.25 \leqslant w < 1.35$, where 1.25 is the **lower bound** and 1.35 kg is the **upper bound**. The **error interval** for w is $1.25 \leqslant w < 1.35$.

1 Given that $x = 2.25$ correct to 2 decimal places and $y = 1.4$ correct to 1 decimal place, find the maximum and minimum values and state the error intervals for

a $x + y$ _____

b $x - y$ _____

c xy _____

d $\dfrac{x}{y}$ _____

2 A card measuring 12.5 cm by 8.5 cm (both measured to the nearest 0.1 cm) is to be posted in an envelope that is 13 cm by 10 cm (both to the nearest 1 cm).

Can you guarantee that the card will fit into the envelope? Explain your answer.

_____

_____

3 Sammi runs a 50 m race at an average speed of 6 m/s.

Both values are measured to an accuracy of 1 significant figure.

a What is Sammi's fastest possible time to complete the race?

_____

Sammi has an average stride length of 1.32 m, to the nearest centimetre.

b What is the smallest number of strides she will take to complete the race?

_____

_____

4 The maximum load a van can carry is 1600 kg to the nearest 10 kg.

The van is to be loaded with boxes of beans. Each box weighs 12 kg to the nearest 0.1 kg.

Assuming the van is large enough, what is the minimum number of boxes of beans it can carry?

_____

_____

5 A rubber brick is in the shape of a cuboid.

The length of the brick is l cm.

The cross section of the brick is a square of side h cm.

The mass of the brick is M kg.

$l = 32$ correct to the nearest centimetre

$M = 3.99$ correct to 2 decimal places

$h = 10.2$ correct to 1 decimal place

Find the density of the rubber correct to an appropriate degree of accuracy.

Give your answer in g/cm³.

Explain why your answer is to an appropriate degree of accuracy.

Hint: $\text{density} = \dfrac{\text{mass}}{\text{volume}}$

_____

_____

_____

_____

1.6 Indices

1 Work out the following.

> **Hint:** When powers of the same number are multiplied or divided, the rules of indices should be followed, i.e. for multiplication add the powers, and for division subtract the powers. For example, $5^5 \times 5^{-2} = 5^{5+-2} = 5^3$ and $2^7 \div 2^{-3} = 2^{7-(-3)} = 2^{10}$.

a $4^4 \times 4^{-2}$ _____

b $4^2 \div 4^{-2}$ _____

c $8^4 \times 8^{-4}$ _____

d $\dfrac{2^5}{2^9}$ _____

2 Find the value of the following.

> **Hint:** Remember: $x^{-n} = \dfrac{1}{x^n}$. Use the rules of indices to simplify,
>
> e.g. $125^{\frac{2}{3}} = \left(125^{\frac{1}{3}}\right)^2 = 5^2 = 25$. Always take the root part (the denominator) first as it makes the number smaller and easier to deal with.

a 1^0 _____

b 4^{-2} _____

c $125^{\frac{1}{3}}$ _____

d $32^{-\frac{1}{5}}$ _____

e $9^{\frac{3}{2}}$ _____

f $\left(\dfrac{81}{16}\right)^{-\frac{3}{4}}$ _____

3 $5 \times \sqrt{125} = 5^n$

Find the value of n. _____

4 $2^x \times 2^y = 128$

and $2^x \div 2^y = 8$

Find the values of x and y. _____

> **Hint:** Write 128 and 8 as powers of 2, then use the rules of indices to form simultaneous equations for x and y.

5 $x = 3^p$, $y = 3^q$

a Express the following in terms of x and/or y.

i 3^{p+q} _____

ii 3^{2p} _____

iii 3^{q-1} _____

$xy = 27$ and $3x^2y = 27$

_____

b Find the value of p and the value of q.

_____

1.7 Recurring decimals to fractions

Hint: Multiply by 10^n using suitable values of n to form a pair of simultaneous equations and find a solution.

1 Convert each of these recurring decimals to a fraction in its simplest form.

Hint: To convert $0.\dot{9}$ to a fraction, start by writing $x = 0.9999...$; hence $10x = 9.9999...$ then you can find the value of $9x$.

a $0.\dot{1}$ _____

b $0.\dot{4}$ _____

_____ _____

_____ _____

2 Ben says that $0.\dot{9}$ is equivalent to 1. Claire thinks he is wrong.

How can Ben use recurring decimals and fractions to show Claire that $0.\dot{9}$ is equivalent to 1?

_____

_____

_____

3 Convert each of these recurring decimals to a fraction in its simplest form.

Hint: Use values of 10^n to form a pair of simultaneous equations, e.g. if $x = 0.1\dot{4}$, find $10x$ and $100x$ to set up the simultaneous equations.

a $0.\dot{2}\dot{3}$ _____

b $0.0\dot{2}$ _____

_____ _____

_____ _____

_____ _____

c $0.24\dot{3}$ _____

d $0.2\dot{2}0\dot{4}$ _____

_____ _____

_____ _____

_____ _____

④ Convert each of these fractions to decimal form.

a $\frac{7}{9}$ _____

b $\frac{41}{45}$ _____

_____

_____

_____

_____

_____

c $\frac{103}{330}$ _____

_____

_____

_____

1.8 Surds

Hint: Remember: identify any square numbers that are factors. $\sqrt{a} \times \sqrt{b} = \sqrt{ab}$ and $\sqrt{\frac{a}{b}} = \frac{\sqrt{a}}{\sqrt{b}}$.

① Write each of these expressions as a single square root in its simplest form.

a $\sqrt{3} \times \sqrt{5}$ _____

b $\sqrt{3} \times \sqrt{2} \times \sqrt{10}$ _____

② Work out the value of each of the following.

a $\sqrt{5} \times \sqrt{5}$ _____

b $\sqrt{3} \times \sqrt{2} \times \sqrt{6}$ _____

c $\sqrt{10} \times \sqrt{40}$ _____

d $\sqrt{6} \times \sqrt{2} \times \sqrt{12}$ _____

e $\sqrt{600} \div \sqrt{6}$ _____

f $\sqrt{63} \div \sqrt{7}$ _____

3 Write the following in the form $a\sqrt{b}$ where b is a prime number.

> **Hint:** Look for square numbers that are factors of the root shown and then use $\sqrt{ab} = \sqrt{a} \times \sqrt{b}$.

a $\sqrt{12}$ _____

b $\sqrt{80}$ _____

4 Simplify these expressions. Write your answers in surd form where necessary.

a $3\sqrt{5} \times 2\sqrt{3}$ _____

b $3\sqrt{8} \times 3\sqrt{3}$ _____

c $\dfrac{4\sqrt{30}}{\sqrt{6}}$ _____

d $\dfrac{8\sqrt{125}}{2\sqrt{20}}$ _____

e $\sqrt{50} + 2\sqrt{32}$ _____

f $6\sqrt{12} - 3\sqrt{27}$ _____

5 Evaluate the following.

> **Hint:** Break down the numerators and denominators into factors and write the surds in their simplest form. Cancel where possible.

a $\dfrac{18}{\sqrt{5}} \times \dfrac{\sqrt{20}}{3}$ _____

b $\dfrac{15\sqrt{70}}{\sqrt{5}} \times \dfrac{2\sqrt{2}}{3\sqrt{7}}$ _____

6 Simplify by rationalising the denominator.

> **Hint:** If a number is multiplied by 1 its value remains the same. Importantly, 1 can be written as $\dfrac{\sqrt{a}}{\sqrt{a}}$. Remember: $\sqrt{a} \times \sqrt{a} = a$.

a $\dfrac{12}{\sqrt{3}}$ _____

b $\dfrac{12}{\sqrt{8}}$ _____

c $\dfrac{3\sqrt{5}}{2\sqrt{45}}$ _____

d $\dfrac{4}{1+\sqrt{3}}$ _____

7 Expand the brackets and simplify.

a $\left(2+\sqrt{3}\right)\left(4+\sqrt{3}\right)$ _____

b $\left(4-3\sqrt{3}\right)\left(5+4\sqrt{3}\right)$ _____

c $\left(1-2\sqrt{7}\right)^{2}$ _____

8 Show that $\left(\sqrt{15}-\sqrt{12}\right)\left(\sqrt{15}+\sqrt{12}\right)=3$.

_____

_____

9 Simplify $\dfrac{8+\sqrt{27}}{4}-\dfrac{2+2\sqrt{3}}{3}$.

_____

_____

10 **a** Show that this triangle is right angled.

_____

_____

Diagram **not** accurately drawn

_____

b Find the exact area of the triangle.

_____

_____

11 Simplify each of the following, rationalising the denominator where necessary.

a $\sqrt{72}$ _____

b $\sqrt{27}\times\sqrt{54}$ _____

c $\dfrac{\sqrt{15}\times\sqrt{35}}{\sqrt{21}}$ _____

d $\dfrac{2\sqrt{5}\times5\sqrt{12}}{5\sqrt{2}}$ _____

e $\dfrac{a\sqrt{5x}-b\sqrt{35x}}{5ab\sqrt{x}}$ _____

2 Algebra

2.1 Solving quadratic equations graphically

1 The diagram shows part of the graph of $y = x^2 + 2x - 3$.

> **Hint:** The roots of a quadratic equation $ax^2 + bx + c = 0$ are the values of x that satisfy the equation. They are the values of x where the graph of $y = ax^2 + bx + c$ crosses the x axis, i.e. where $y = 0$. If the graph does not cross the x axis, then the quadratic equation has no real roots.

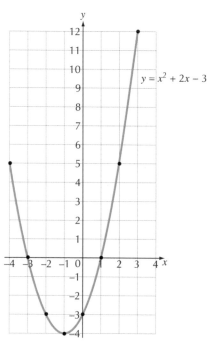

$y = x^2 + 2x - 3$

a Write down the roots of the equation $x^2 + 2x - 3 = 0$.

_____

b Write down the equation of the line of symmetry for the graph of $y = x^2 + 2x - 3$.

_____

c By drawing a suitable straight line, use your graph to find estimates for the solutions of $x^2 + x - 5 = 0$.

> **Hint:** Rearrange the equation as $x^2 + 2x - 3 = ax + b$ and find the values of a and b. The equation of the line to draw is $y = ax + b$.

_____

_____

P is the point on the graph where $x = 0$.

d Calculate an estimate for the gradient of the graph at the point P.

> Hint: The gradient of a curve at any point is the same as the gradient of the tangent to the curve at that point.

_____

_____

 2 The diagram shows part of the graph of $y = 5 + 2x - x^2$.

a Write down the coordinates of the maximum point.

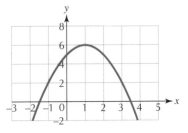

_____

_____

b Write down estimates for the roots of the equation $5 + 2x - x^2 = 0$.

_____

c Show that the equation $5 + 2x - x^2 = 0$ can be rearranged to give $x = \sqrt{2x + 5}$.

_____

d Use the iteration $x_{n+1} = \sqrt{2x_n + 5}$, with $x_0 = 3$, to find the positive root of the equation $5 + 2x - x^2 = 0$ to 3, decimal places.

> Hint: Use the ANS key on your calculator: key in '3''=' then '$\sqrt{2 \times \text{ANS} + 5}$''=''=' ... to find the values of x_1, x_2, x_3 etc. Continue until two successive values agree to 3 decimal places.

_____

_____

_____

2.2 Recognising shapes of graphs

> Hint: Match the obvious ones first.

Match each graph with its equation.

1 $y = 2x^2 + 4$ is graph _____

2 $y = x^2 + 2x$ is graph _____

3 $y = 2x + 4$ is graph _____

4 $y = x^3 + 4$ is graph _____

5 $y = -x^3 + 4$ is graph _____

6 $y = x^2 + 2x + 4$ is graph _____

7 $y = \dfrac{4}{x}$ is graph _____

8 $y = 3^x$ is graph _____

9 $y = \cos x$ is graph _____

10 $y = \sin x$ is graph _____

A

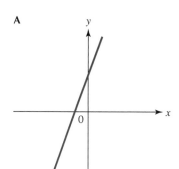

B

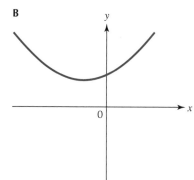

C

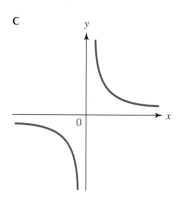

D

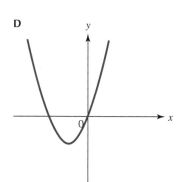

E

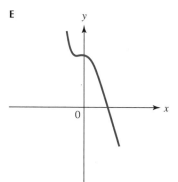

F

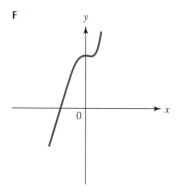

G

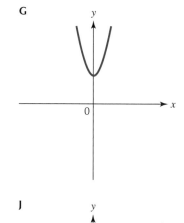

H

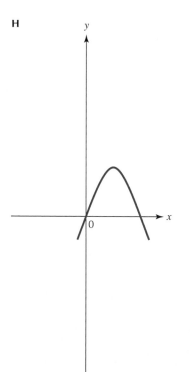

I

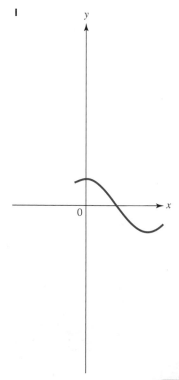

J

2.3 Real-life graphs

1 The graph shows the velocity–time graph for a train journey.

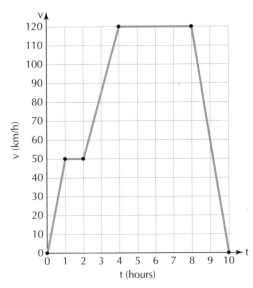

Work out:

a the acceleration in the first hour

_____

b the deceleration in the last hour

_____

c the acceleration between $t = 2$ and $t = 4$ hours

_____

d the distance travelled in the first two hours

_____

_____

e the distance travelled in the last two hours.

_____

_____

2 Abby invested £1000 in an account that paid 9% compound interest per annum.

The interest is added to the account at the end of each year.

Abby left the money in the account for 15 years.

She did not add or withdraw any money from the account in this time.

> **Hint:** Remember that for compound interest the amount of interest will change each year.

a Explain why the amount of money, A, in the account at the end of n years can be written as $A = 1000 \times 1.09^n$.

_____

_____

_____

_____

b Draw the graph of $A = 1000 \times 1.09^n$ for $0 \leqslant n \leqslant 15$.

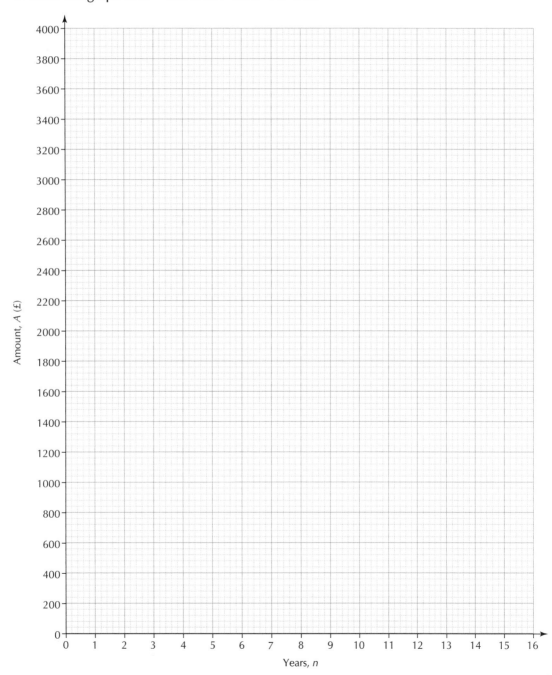

c Use your graph to find the number of years it took for the initial amount Abby invested to triple in value.

_____

Hint: You can check your answer by substituting into the formula for compound interest.

 3 The velocity-time graph shows the velocity in m/s of a car in the first 10 seconds of its motion.

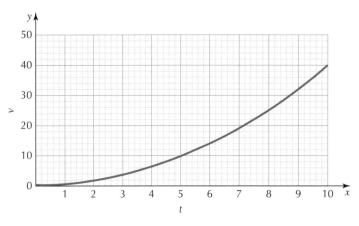

a Describe how the acceleration of the car changes over the first 10 seconds.

_____

_____

b Estimate the acceleration of the car at time $t = 4$ seconds.

_____

_____

c Use five equal strips on the graph to estimate the distance travelled by the car in the first 10 seconds.

Hint: Divide the area under the graph into a triangle and 4 trapezia and work out the total area.

Area of trapezium $= \frac{1}{2}h(a + b)$

_____

_____

d Is your answer to part **c** an overestimate or an underestimate? You must justify your answer.

Hint: Consider where the lines of the shapes lie in relation to the curve.

_____

_____

e The distance travelled in the first 10 seconds can be estimated using 10 equal strips on the graph.

Comment on the effect this would have on your answer for the distance travelled. You must justify your answer.

_____

_____

2.4 Straight lines and their equations 🖩

Hint: The equation of a straight line can be written in the form $y = mx + c$, where m is the gradient and c is the intercept on the y axis.

The gradient, m, of the line joining the points (x_1, y_1) and (x_2, y_2) is given by $m = \dfrac{y_2 - y_1}{x_2 - x_1}$.

The coordinates of the midpoint of the line joining the points (x_1, y_1) and (x_2, y_2) are $\left(\dfrac{x_1 + x_2}{2}, \dfrac{y_1 + y_2}{2} \right)$.

1 For the line joining the points (−3, 1) and (2, −3), work out:

a the gradient

_____

b the coordinates of the midpoint.

_____

_____

2 **a** Work out the equation of the line with gradient $\dfrac{1}{2}$ that passes through the point (6, −1).

Hint: The equation of a line with gradient, m, that passes through the point (x_1, y_1) is $y - y_1 = m(x - x_1)$.

_____

_____

_____

_____

b Work out the equation of the line that is perpendicular to the line $3x - 2y + 7 = 0$ and passes through the point $(-2, 1)$.

> **Hint:** To find the gradient, m, of a straight line write it in the form $y = mx + c$. Parallel lines have the same gradient. If two lines with gradients m_1 and m_2 are perpendicular, then $m_2 = -\dfrac{1}{m_1}$.

_____

_____

3 For the points A $(2, 1)$ and B $(6, -7)$ find:

a the exact length of AB

> **Hint:** The length of the line joining the points (x_1, y_1) and (x_2, y_2) is $\sqrt{(x_2 - x_1)^2 + (y_2 - y_1)^2}$.

_____

_____

_____

_____

b the equation of the line that passes through A and B

> **Hint:** To find the equation of a line that passes through two given points, first find the gradient, m, then use $y - y_1 = m(x - x_1)$ using one of the points the line passes through.

_____

_____

c the equation of the perpendicular bisector of AB.

_____

_____

_____

4 The coordinates of the vertices of a triangle are $(0, 4)$, $(2, 1)$ and $(8, 5)$.

Show that the triangle is right angled.

> **Hint:** Use Pythagoras' theorem.

_____

_____

_____

_____

2.5 Equations of circles and their graphs ▦

1 The diagram shows a circle on a Cartesian grid. The point A $(4, 2)$ lies on the circumference of the circle.

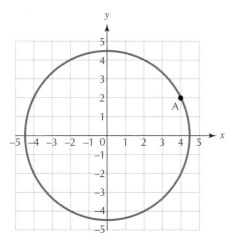

a Work out the exact value of the radius of the circle.

_____

_____

b Write down the equation of the circle.

_____

_____

2 The diagram shows a circle with centre $(0, 0)$ and radius 3.
The point A $(x, -2)$ lies on the circumference.

a Work out the exact value of x.

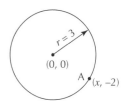

_____

_____

b A larger circle is drawn with centre $(0, 0)$ and radius 4. Work out the exact values of the y coordinates for the two points A and B which both have an x coordinate of -2.

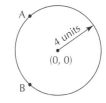

_____

_____

_____

_____

3 The equation of a circle, C, is $x^2 + y^2 = 25$.

The circle is translated by the vector $\begin{pmatrix} 3 \\ 2 \end{pmatrix}$ to give circle B. Draw a sketch of circle B.

Label with coordinates the centre of circle B and any points of intersection with the y axis.

4 The equation of circle C is $x^2 + y^2 = 34$.

a Verify that the point A (5, −3) lies on the circumference of the circle.

_____

_____

b Work out an equation of the tangent to the circle, C, at the point A.

_____

_____

_____

_____

5 C is a circle with equation $x^2 + y^2 = 9$.

$P\left(\dfrac{4}{3}, \dfrac{2\sqrt{14}}{3}\right)$ is a point on C.

Find an equation of the tangent to C at the point P.

_____

_____

_____

2.6 Functions

Hint: You can use function notation to express a rule connecting two or more variables.
For example, $f(x) = 2x^2$ where f is the function and $f(x)$ is read 'f of x'.

1 Given that $f(x) = 3x^2 + 2x$ and $g(x) = \dfrac{4}{x}$, work out:

a $f(3) + g(2)$

_____

b $\dfrac{2f(2)}{g(8)}$

_____

2 If $f(x) = 2x^3 - 6$ and $g(x) = \dfrac{4}{x^2}$, find k given that:

a $f(k) = 48$

_____

b $2g(k) = 32$

_____

3 If $f(x) = 3 - 2x$, $g(x) = x^2$ and $h(x) = \dfrac{2}{x}$, find the following composite functions.

Hint: fg is a composite function. To find $fg(x)$, first work out $g(x)$ then substitute the output into $f(x)$.
For example, $f(x) = 3x^2$, $g(x) = 2x - 1$ then $fg(x) = f[2x - 1] = 3(2x - 1)^2$. Note that $fg(x)$ is not the same as $gf(x)$, $gf(x) = g[3x^2] = 2(3x^2) - 1 = 6x^2 - 1$.

a $fg(x)$

_____

b $gf(x)$

_____

c $fgh(x)$

_____

d $ff(x)$

_____

Evaluate:

e $fg(4)$

Hint: Work out the result for the first function and substitute into the second function.

_____

f $gf(-2)$

_____

g $fgh[8]$

_____

h ff(−1)

_____

 4 Find the inverse of each of the following functions.

> Hint: $f^{-1}(x)$ is the inverse function for $f(x)$, which means that if $f(a) = b$, then $f^{-1}(b) = a$.
> For example, if $f(x) = 3x - 1$, then let $y = 3x - 1$ and make x the subject so
> $3x = y + 1$ means $x = \dfrac{y + 1}{3}$. Replace y by x to give $f^{-1}(x) = \dfrac{x + 1}{3}$.

a $f(x) = 2x + 5$

_____

b $g(x) = \dfrac{x - 1}{4}$

_____

c $h(x) = \sqrt{x - 3}$

_____

 5 $f(x) = \dfrac{x}{x + 3}$ $x \in \mathbb{R}, x \neq -3$

> Hint: $x \in \mathbb{R}$ means x is contained in the set of real numbers.

a Explain why the function is only valid provided $x \neq -3$.

_____

b Find the value(s) of x for which $f(x) = f^{-1}(x)$.

_____

2.7 Inequalities

> Hint: Use dashed lines for inequalities that involve $<$ or $>$. Used full lines for inequalities that involve $\leqslant$ or $\geqslant$.

1 **a** Calculate the area of the region bordered by the inequalities $y \geqslant -2$, $y \leqslant 2x + 1$ and $2x + y \leqslant 5$.

_____

_____

b The region in part **a** is translated by the vector $\begin{pmatrix} 2 \\ 2 \end{pmatrix}$. Work out the inequalities that border the new region.

_____

_____

2 Write down the three inequalities that define the shaded region.

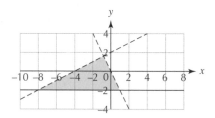

_____

_____

_____

3 Draw graphs to show the region defined by these three inequalities. Shade the region.

$y > 3x - 2$, $y \leqslant x + 3$ and $y > 2$

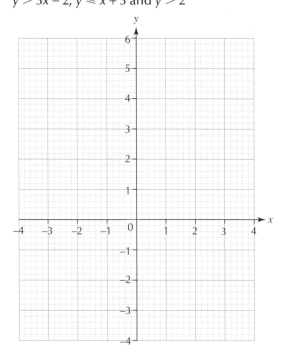

4 **a** Using the grid below, draw the graphs of $xy = 8$ and $x + y = 8$.

b Use your graphs to find all pairs of positive integers with a product greater than 8 and a sum less than 8.

_____

_____

_____

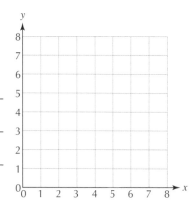

c Explain your answer to part **b** using inequalities.

_____

_____

d Find the exact values of the coordinates of the points of intersection of the curve $xy = 8$ and the line $x + y = 8$.

_____

_____

2.8 Drawing complex graphs

1

a Complete the table of values for the function $y = x^3 + 2x^2 - 1$.

x	-2.5	-2	-1	0	1	1.2
x^3		-8		0	1	
$+2x^2$		8		0	2	
-1		-1		-1	-1	
$y = x^3 + 2x^2 - 1$		-1		-1	2	

b Draw the graph of $y = x^3 + 2x^2 - 1$ for $-2.5 \leqslant x \leqslant 1.2$.

> **Hint:** The graph should be a smooth curve – don't use a ruler.

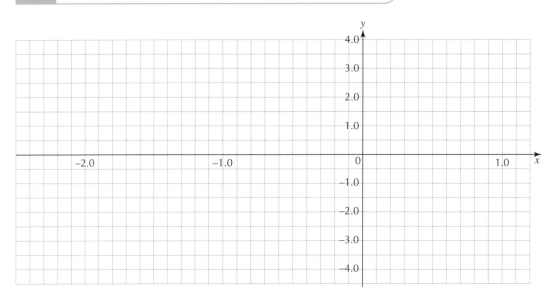

c State the roots of the equation $x^3 + 2x^2 - 1 = 0$.

_____

_____

d Use your graph to find the number of solutions for the equation $x^3 + 2x^2 = 0$. Explain your answer.

_____

_____

2

a Complete the table of values for the function $f(x) = \dfrac{12}{x} + 2$.

x	-6	-5	-4	-3	-2	-1		1	2	3	4	5	6
$f(x)$	0	-0.4			-4			14			5		

b Draw the graph of $f(x) = \dfrac{12}{x} + 2$ for $-6 \leqslant x \leqslant 6$.

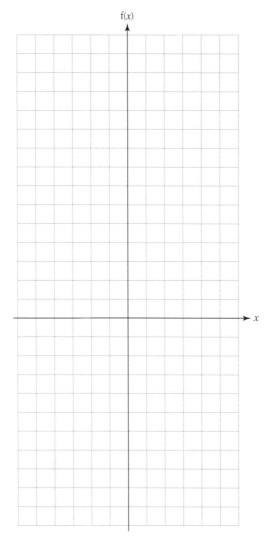

c Write down the equations of the two asymptotes for the graph of $f(x) = \dfrac{12}{x} + 2$.

_____

d Use your graph to estimate the value of $f(3.2)$.

_____

3 The number of *E. coli* bacteria is known to double in size every 20 minutes.

The number of *E. coli* bacteria, N, in a particular colony can be modelled using

$N = 200 \times 2^t$

where t is the number of 20-minute periods of time.

a What does 200 represent in this equation?

_____

b Complete the table of values for the function $N = 200 \times 2^t$.

t	0	1	2	3	4	5	6	8	10	12
N										

c Draw the graph of $N = 200 \times 2^t$ for $0 \leqslant t \leqslant 12$.

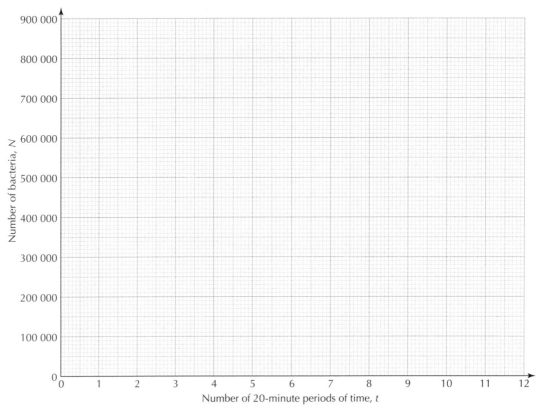

Number of bacteria, N

Number of 20-minute periods of time, t

d Use the graph to estimate the number of bacteria after:

    i   2 hours 10 minutes _____   **ii**   3 hours 10 minutes _____

e Use the graph to estimate the time taken for the number of bacteria to reach:

    i   100 000 _____   **ii**   300 000 _____

f Explain what effect it would have on your answers to parts **d** and **e** if the number of bacteria doubled in size every 15 minutes.

_____

_____

2.9 Areas beneath graphs

1   The diagram shows the graphs of $y = x^2 - 3x + 1$ and $y = x + 1$.

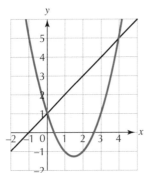

a Write down the coordinates of the point on the curve $y = x^2 - 3x + 1$ where a translation of the line $y = x + 1$ forms a tangent.

_____

_____

_____

b Calculate the gradient of the tangent to the curve at the point (3, 1).

_____

_____

_____

c Work out the area bounded by the graph of $y = x + 1$, the x axis and the lines $x = 0$ and $x = 4$.

_____

_____

_____

2 The diagram shows the graph of $y = 4x - x^2$.

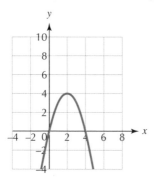

a Write down the coordinates of the maximum point on the graph.

_____

_____

_____

b Use two equal strips on the graph to estimate the area bounded by the curve and the x axis.

_____

_____

_____

3 The velocity–time graph shows a car travelling between two sets of traffic lights.

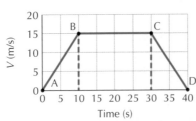

a Explain what is happening to the car between:

  i A and B

_____

  ii B and C

_____

  iii C and D

_____

b Calculate the total distance travelled by the car.

_____

_____

_____

4 The diagram shows the graph of $y = x^2 - x - 2$.

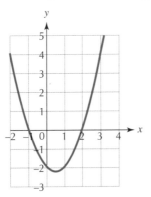

a Use three equal strips on the graph to estimate the area bounded by the curve and the x axis.

_____

_____

_____

b Is your answer to part **a** an overestimate or an underestimate? Explain your answer.

_____

c Explain how you could find a more accurate estimate for the area.

_____

2.10 Trigonometric graphs 📱

These are the graphs of $y = \sin x$ and $y = \cos x$ for $0° \leqslant x \leqslant 360°$.

> **Hint:** The graphs repeat the same shape every 360°, this is called the period of the graphs.

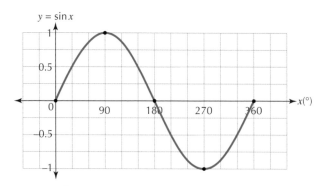
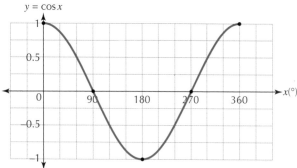

1 Use the graphs above to help you find the solutions to the following equations.

Solve the equations for all values of x to the nearest degree in the interval 0° to 360°.

> **Hint:** Make sure your calculator is in degrees mode. If $\sin x = k$, then $x = \sin^{-1} k$.
> Use the symmetrical properties of the graph to help you find the solutions.

a $\sin x = 0.5878$ _____

b $\cos x = -0.5878$ _____

c $\cos x = 0.0348$ _____

2 $\sin 29° = 0.4848$.

a Find all values of x in the interval $0° \leqslant x \leqslant 360°$ that satisfy the equation $\sin x = -0.4848$.

_____

_____

b Find all the solutions of the equation $\cos x = 0.4848$ in the interval $0° \leqslant x \leqslant 360°$.

_____

_____

3 Plot the graphs of $y = \cos x$ and $y = \sin x$ on the same axes for $0 \leqslant x \leqslant 360°$.

  a Use your graphs to estimate the values of x for which $\sin x = \cos x$ for $0 \leqslant x \leqslant 360°$. Use a calculator to check your answers.

_____

_____

  b Work out the solutions for which $\sin x = \cos x$ for $-180 \leqslant x \leqslant 720°$.

_____

_____

4 Solve the equation $5 \sin x = 3.5$ for values of x in the interval $0° \leqslant x \leqslant 720°$.

> **Hint:** To solve equations of the form $a \sin x = b$ or $a \cos x = b$, first rearrange the equations as $\sin x = \dfrac{b}{a}$ or $\cos x = \dfrac{b}{a}$. Use a calculator to find the first solution, and then use a sketch of the graph $y = \sin x$ or $y = \cos x$ and symmetry to find the other solutions.

_____

_____

5 Solve the equation $12 \cos \theta = -5.2$ for values of θ in the interval $0° \leqslant x \leqslant 720°$.

_____

_____

6 This is the graph of $y = \tan x$ for $0 \leqslant x \leqslant 360°$.

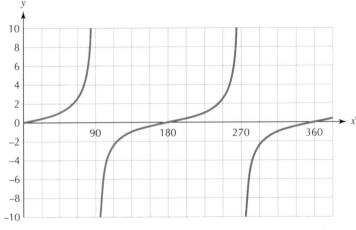

  a What is the period of the graph?

_____

Hint: You need to know the exact values of these trig functions.

	0°	30°	45°	60°	90°
sin	0	$\dfrac{1}{2}$	$\dfrac{\sqrt{2}}{2}$	$\dfrac{\sqrt{3}}{2}$	1
cos	1	$\dfrac{\sqrt{3}}{2}$	$\dfrac{\sqrt{2}}{2}$	$\dfrac{1}{2}$	0
tan	0	$\dfrac{\sqrt{3}}{3}$	1	$\sqrt{3}$	

b Without using a calculator, find all solutions of the equation $\tan x = \sqrt{3}$ for $0° \leqslant x \leqslant 720°$.

_____

_____

2.11 Transformation of functions

1 This is the graph of the function $y = \sin x$.

Match these transformations of the function $y = \sin x$ with its graph.

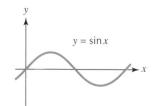

a $y = \sin(2x + 1) = $ _____

b $y = 2\sin x = $ _____

c $y = -\sin(2x + 1) = $ _____

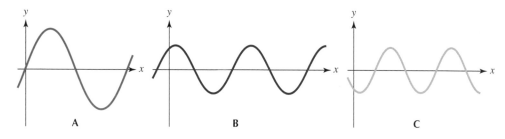

A   B   C

2 The graph of the function $y = \cos x$ is labelled. Identify and label the other four functions shown.

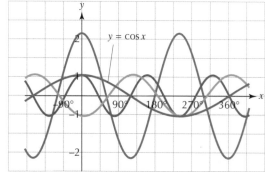

3 The graph shows the function $y = f(x)$.

Write down the coordinates of the points A, B and C under these transformations.

a $2f(x)$: A (____, ____), B (____, ____), C (____, ____)

b $-3f(x)$: A (____, ____), B (____, ____), C (____, ____)

c $\frac{1}{2}f(x)$: A (____, ____), B (____, ____), C (____, ____)

d $2f(x-2)$: A (____, ____), B (____, ____), C (____, ____)

e $2f(x)+1$: A (____, ____), B (____, ____), C (____, ____)

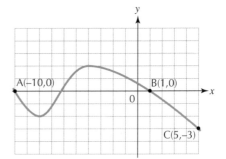

4 The graph shows the function $y = f(x)$.

Write down the coordinates of the points A, B and C under these transformations.

a $f(x) - 5$:

A (____, ____), B (____, ____), C (____, ____)

b $2 + f(x)$:

A (____, ____), B (____, ____), C (____, ____)

5 Look at the graph of $y = f(x)$ above.

Write down the coordinates of the points A, B and C under these transformations.

a $f(2x)$: A (____, ____), B (____, ____), C (____, ____)

b $f(-x)$: A (____, ____), B (____, ____), C (____, ____)

c $f\left(\frac{1}{2}x\right)$: A(____, ____), B (____, ____), C (____, ____)

6 This is the graph of the function $y = \cos x$.

Use different colours to draw these graphs.

a $y = \cos x + 1$

b $y = \cos 2x$

c $y = -\cos x$

d $y = 2\cos x$

e $y = 1 - \cos(x - 90°)$

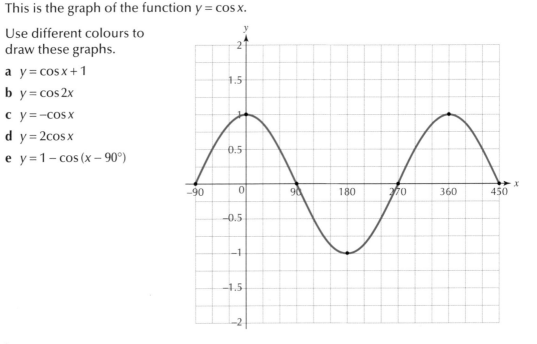

2 Algebra

2.12 Changing the subject of a formula

Hint: Make sure you show each step of your working.

1 Make r the subject of each of the following formulae.

a $f = \sqrt{3r - e}$

b $V = \frac{1}{3}\pi r^2 h$

c $T = 2\pi\sqrt{\dfrac{r}{g}}$

2 Make x the subject of each of the following formulae.

a $tx + y = 7 - tx$

b $4(x - y) = 2x + 3$

c $a(x + r) = b(x + t)$

3 Make x the subject of each of the following formulae.

a $\sqrt{\dfrac{3x + a}{x}} = b$

b $ax^2 + b = t - cx^2$

c $\dfrac{a}{b} = \dfrac{x}{c(d - x)}$

4 Make the following the subject of the formula $x = \dfrac{y^2}{r} - \dfrac{1}{r}$.

a r

b y

2.13 Solving simultaneous equations: one linear, one non-linear

1 Solve each pair of simultaneous equations graphically.

a $y = x^2 - 2x$
$y = x + 4$

b $y = 2x^2$
$y = 2x + 4$

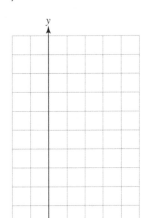

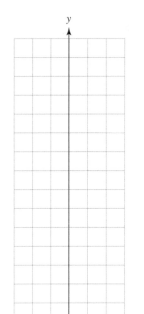

a $x =$ _____ $y =$ _____   **b** $x =$ _____ $y =$ _____

   $x =$ _____ $y =$ _____ $x =$ _____ $y =$ _____

2 Solve algebraically the following simultaneous equations.

$y = x^2 - 4x + 8$
$y = 16 - 2x$

> **Hint:** Use substitution to solve these simultaneous equations.

_____

_____

_____

_____

_____

3 This is Mark's solution to the following pair of simultaneous equations. The solution is incorrect. Where did he make his mistake?

$y = x^2 + 6x + 4$

$y = 2x + 1$

$\therefore 2x + 1 = x^2 + 6x + 4$

$\therefore 0 = x^2 + 4x + 4$

'I now complete the square.'

$x^2 + 4x = -3$

$(x + 2)^2 = -3$

$\sqrt{(x + 2)^2} = \sqrt{-3}$

'It is not possible to find the square root of a negative number so there are no solutions to this problem.'

_____

_____

4 C is the curve with equation $x^2 + y^2 = 29$.

L is the line with equation $y = x - 7$.

L intersects C at two points A and B.

Calculate the exact length of AB.

_____

_____

_____

5 This is Clotilde's solution to the following pair of simultaneous equations. The solution is incorrect. Where did she make her mistake?

$x^2 + y^2 = 13$ (a)

$y - x = 1$ (b)

'Make 'y' the subject in (b)'

$y = x + 1$

'Substitute this into (a).'

$x^2 + (x + 1)^2 = 13$

$\therefore x^2 + x^2 + 2x + 1 = 13$

$\therefore 2x^2 + 2x - 12 = 0$

'Now factorise this to find x.'

$2(x^2 + x - 6) = 0$

$\therefore 2(x + 6)(x - 1) = 0$

$\therefore x = 1, y = 2$ or $x = -6, y = -5$

_____

_____

6 A straight line has equation $y = 3x + 2$.

A curve has equation $y^2 = -12(x + 1)$.

a Solve the simultaneous equations algebraically.

_____

_____

_____

_____

_____

_____

_____

_____

_____

_____

_____

b Here are three sketches showing the curve $y^2 = -12(x + 1)$ and three possible positions of the line $y = 3x + 2$.

Sketch 1 **Sketch 2** **Sketch 3**

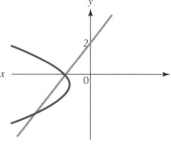

Which is the correct sketch? Give a reason for your choice.

_____

_____

_____

_____

_____

_____

2.14 Solving quadratic equations

Solve the following quadratic equations by factorising.

1 $2x^2 + 7x = 15$

_____

_____

_____

2 $12x^2 + 5x = 2$

_____

_____

_____

3 $7x^2 - 6x - 60 = x^2 + 4x - 4$

_____

_____

_____

4   The following quadratic equation was solved by factorising, but it is incorrect. Where is/are the mistake(s)?

$2x^2 + 7x + 3 = 0$

$2x^2 + 6x + x + 3 = 0$

$(2x^2 + 6x) + (x + 3) = 0$

$2x(x + 3) + 1(x + 3) = 0$

$\therefore (x + 3)(2x + 1) = 0$

$\therefore x = \dfrac{1}{2} \quad \text{or} \quad x = -3$

5   Solve $9(x + 1) = \dfrac{28}{x}$.

_____

_____

_____

_____

6 The diagram shows a triangle and a rectangle. The sum of both areas is equal to 46 cm². Calculate the value of x.

 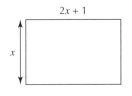

_____

_____

_____

_____

7 Solve $\dfrac{1}{x+1} + \dfrac{2}{4-x} = \dfrac{9}{4}$.

_____

_____

_____

_____

_____

_____

_____

2.15 Solving quadratic equations: using $x = \dfrac{-b \pm \sqrt{b^2 - 4ac}}{2a}$

1 Solve these quadratic equations, giving your answers correct to 2 decimal places.

a $5x^2 + 2x = 9$

_____

_____

_____

_____

_____

b $x^2 + 9 = 3x + 14$

_____

_____

_____

_____

2 Solve $3x - 2 - x^2 = x^2 - x - 5$, giving your answers in surd form.

_____

_____

_____

_____

_____

3 Find the exact solutions of $3x - \dfrac{4}{x} = 2$.

_____

_____

_____

2.16 Completing the square 🖩

Hint: A quadratic can be written in completed square form, $y = a(x + b)^2 + c$, where the coordinates of the turning point are $(-b, c)$.

1 Write each expression in the form $(x + p)^2 + q$, where p and q are constants.

a $x^2 + 4x - 6$ **b** $x^2 - 20x - 1$ **c** $x^2 - 5x - 0.5$

_____ _____ _____

_____ _____ _____

_____ _____ _____

2 Solve each quadratic equation by completing the square.

a $x^2 - 8x = -13$ **b** $3x^2 - 4 = 2x^2 - 3x + 4$

_____ _____

_____ _____

_____ _____

_____ _____

_____ _____

3 **a** Write $2x^2 - 6x - 1$ in the form $a(x + b)^2 + c$, and hence write down the coordinates of the turning point of $y = 2x^2 - 6x - 1$.

_____

_____

b State the range in values for y.

_____

_____

c Work out the roots of $y = 2x^2 - 6x - 1$ in surd form.

_____

_____

d Where does the graph of $y = 2x^2 - 6x - 1$ cross the y axis?

_____

_____

e Use your answers to parts **a** to **d** to sketch the graph of $y = 2x^2 - 6x - 1$.

> **Hint:** When you draw a sketch of a graph, make sure you include the coordinates of the key points.

4 **a** Write $3x^2 - 6x + 10$ in the form $a(x + b)^2 + c$.

_____

_____

b Write down the equation of the line of symmetry for the graph of $y = 3x^2 - 6x + 10$.

_____

_____

c Explain why there are no solutions for the equation $3x^2 - 6x + 10 = 0$.

_____

_____

5 For the graph of the equation $y = x^2 + 2x + 3$.

a Find the minimum value of y.

_____

_____

b Explain why $x^2 + 2x + 3 = 0$ has no real roots.

> **Hint:** Complete the square for the expression $x^2 + 2x + 3$ and use this to describe the position of the graph in relation to the x axis.

_____

_____

_____

c Find the set of values that satisfy the inequality $x^2 - 2x - 15 \geqslant 0$.

> **Hint:** Find the roots of the equation $x^2 - 2x - 15 = 0$, sketch the graph of $y = x^2 - 2x - 15$ and use this to find the set of values of x.

_____

_____

_____

2.17 Solving inequalities

1 The net of a tetrahedron is shown.

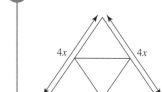

a Work out the total length of the edges, E, of the tetrahedron in terms of x.

_____

_____

b Work out the total surface area, A, of the tetrahedron in terms of x.

_____

_____

c Work out the minimum value of x such that $A \geqslant E$.

_____

_____

_____

② A is an equilateral triangle and B is
an isosceles triangle.

a Prove that the area of A can never be
greater than the area of B.

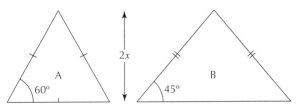

_____

_____

b Calculate the maximum value of x such that perimeter of A $\geqslant$ area of B.

_____

_____

c Calculate the range of values of x such that area of A $<$ perimeter of B.

_____

_____

③ Find the set of possible values of x that satisfy the inequality $x^2 - 2x - 15 \geqslant 0$.

Hint: A solution such as $x > a$ can be written in set notation as $\{x: x > a\}$ which
means the set of all x values such that $x > a$.

Graph of $y = ax^2 + bx + c$

$a > 0$

$ax^2 + bx + c > 0$

$y > 0$

Solutions $x < x_1$ and $x > x_2$

$\{x: x < x_1 \cup x > x_2\}$

$ax^2 + bx + c < 0$

$y < 0$

Solution $x_1 < x < x_2$

$\{x: x_1 < x < x_2\}$

_____

_____

4 Find the set of possible values of x that satisfy $2x^2 - 5x - 7 > 0$. Give your answer in set notation.

_____

_____

5 Find the exact form for the set of possible values of x that satisfy the inequality $9x^2 + 9x - 10 \leqslant 0$.

_____

_____

_____

2.18 Simplifying algebraic fractions

Hint: Factorise the numerator and/or the denominator and cancel where possible.

1 Simplify the following.

a $\dfrac{x^2 + 8x + 7}{x + 1}$ _____

_____

b $\dfrac{30x^2y^2 - 2x}{15xy^2 - 1}$ _____

_____

c $\dfrac{x^2 - 2x - 8}{x^2 + 5x + 6}$ _____

_____

d $\dfrac{x - 4}{x^2 - 16}$ _____

_____

e $\dfrac{2x^2 - 5x + 2}{6x^2 - 7x + 2}$ _____

_____

f $\dfrac{10x^2 + 20x - 30}{2x^2 + 10x + 12}$ _____

_____

2.19 Simplifying algebraic fractions (addition and subtraction)

> **Hint:** You need to express the terms as a single fraction with a common denominator, as for normal fractions.

 1 Simplify the following.

a $\dfrac{2c + 4}{2} - \dfrac{3c - 3}{5}$ _____

b $\dfrac{7}{d} + \dfrac{3}{e}$ _____

2 Find and simplify an expression for the perimeter of the rectangle.

_____

_____

_____

_____

3 Simplify the following.

a $\dfrac{1}{x - 3} - \dfrac{2}{x - 5}$ _____

b $\dfrac{10}{x - 5} + \dfrac{2}{(x - 5)^2}$ _____

c $\dfrac{2}{x - 9} + \dfrac{3}{x + 9}$ _____

4 Find the difference between the perimeters of the two triangles.

_____

_____

_____

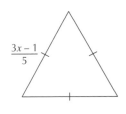

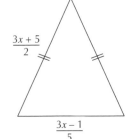

5 $2 - \dfrac{x - 1}{x + 2} - \dfrac{x + 5}{x - 2}$ can be written as a single fraction in the form $\dfrac{px + q}{x^2 - 4}$, where p and q are integers. Work out the value of p and the value of q.

_____

_____

2.20 Simplifying algebraic fractions (multiplication and division)

1 Simplify the following.

a $\dfrac{x}{y^2} \times \dfrac{y^3}{5x}$ _____

b $\dfrac{x}{y^2} \div \dfrac{y^3}{5x}$ _____

c $\dfrac{80a}{16}$ _____

d $\dfrac{20a^2}{4a}$ _____

2 Simplify the following.

a $\dfrac{x^2 - 9x + 18}{15} \div \dfrac{x^2 - x - 30}{25}$ _____

_____

b $\dfrac{t + 5}{4} \times \dfrac{t^2 - 4t}{t^2 + 5t}$ _____

c $\dfrac{x^2}{x^2 + 3} \div \dfrac{x}{x + 3}$ _____

3 Simplify the following.

a $\dfrac{x^2 - 16}{7} \times \dfrac{21}{x^2 - 6x + 8}$ _____

_____

b $\dfrac{x^2 - 4x}{3x^2 + 2x - 8} \div \dfrac{3x^2 - 16x + 16}{x^2 - 2x - 8}$ _____

_____

_____

_____

2.21 Solving equations with algebraic fractions ▤

Hint: You need to express the terms with the same denominator as for normal fractions.

Solve the following equations.

1 $\dfrac{x - 2}{2} + \dfrac{x + 1}{3} = 4$

_____

_____

_____

_____

2 $\dfrac{x-3}{5} - \dfrac{x-2}{3} = 5$

3 $\dfrac{x+2}{5} - \dfrac{2x-1}{4} = 4$

4 $\dfrac{2x-5}{3} - \dfrac{3x-8}{5} = 3$

5 $\dfrac{x}{3} + \dfrac{4x+3}{6} = 7\dfrac{1}{2}$

6 Solve $\dfrac{x+2}{3} - \dfrac{2x+1}{4} = -5$.

7 Solve $\dfrac{3}{2x-1} + \dfrac{3}{4} = 1$.

_____

_____

_____

_____

_____

2.22 Identities and proof

1 1, 3, 6, 10, 15 are the first five triangular numbers. Prove that the sum of the nth and $(n+1)$th triangular numbers is equal to the $(n+1)$th square number.

_____

_____

_____

_____

2 Prove algebraically that the sum of two consecutive odd numbers is always a multiple of 4.

_____

_____

_____

_____

3 Prove that the difference between the squares of any two consecutive integers is equal to the sum of the two integers.

_____

_____

_____

_____

4 Show that $(2x - 3)^3 \equiv ax^3 + bx^2 + cx + d$.

> Hint: The symbol $\equiv$ means 'is equivalent to'. To expand $(ax + b)^3$, write as $(ax + b)(ax + b)^2$, and then expand $(ax + b)^2$ first: $(ax + b)^2 = a^2x^2 + 2abx + b^2$; then multiply by $(ax + b)$, i.e. $ax(a^2x^2 + 2abx + b^2) + b(a^2x^2 + 2abx + b^2)$.

_____

_____

_____

_____

5 Show that $\dfrac{1}{x^2 + x} - \dfrac{1}{x^2 - 2x} \equiv \dfrac{A}{x(x + 1)(x - 2)}$ and find the value of A.

_____

_____

_____

_____

6 Show that $(2n + 1)^3 - (2n - 1)^3$ can be written in the form $an^2 + b$ and find the values of a and b.

_____

_____

_____

_____

_____

2.23 Sequences and iteration

> Hint: If in a sequence of numbers the first differences are the same, then the nth term is of the form $an + b$, where a is the difference between the terms and b is the 'zero term'. This is called an **arithmetic** sequence.

1 Circle the expression for the nth term of the following sequence.

-12 $\quad -3 \quad$ $6 \quad$ $15 \quad$ 24

$12n + 9$ $\qquad$ $9n - 21$ $\qquad$ $9n$ $\qquad$ $9 - 12n$

2 Here is a sequence:

$$3 \quad \frac{5}{2} \quad \frac{7}{3} \quad \frac{9}{4} \quad \frac{11}{5}$$

a Find the next term in the sequence.

_____

b Find an expression for the *n*th term for the sequence.

> Hint: In a sequence of numbers, see if you can find a relationship between the position of the term and, in this example, the value of the numerator and the value of the denominator to work out an expression for the *n*th term.

_____

c Find the product of the 7th and 10th terms.

_____

_____

_____

3 Work out the general term for the following sequence and hence calculate the 12th term.

$$\sqrt{2} \quad \frac{\sqrt{3}}{2} \quad \frac{2}{3} \quad \frac{\sqrt{5}}{4} \quad \frac{\sqrt{6}}{5}$$

_____

_____

4 Given that $u_n = (n+1)(n-1)$, work out the first five terms in the sequence, u_1, u_2, u_3, u_4, u_5.

> Hint: The first term, u_1, is the value you get when you substitute $n = 1$ into the expression for u_n.

_____

_____

5 **a** Write down the next two terms in the Fibonacci sequence 3, 5, 8, 13, ….

_____

b Show that the sum of the first six terms of the sequence is 4 times the fifth number in the sequence.

> Hint: A Fibonacci sequence is a sequence where the next term in the sequence is the sum of the two previous terms.

_____

_____

6 $u_n = (n + 2)^2 - 4$.

a Work out the first five terms in the sequence, u_1, u_2, u_3, u_4, u_5.

b Work out the position of the term that is equal to 525.

7 Fifty-two playing cards are arranged next to each other. One grain of salt was placed on the first card, then double this on the second and double this on the third and so on, so that each card had twice the number of grains as the previous one.

a Work out the nth term for this sequence.

b How many grains of salt should be placed on the last card?

8 The first five terms in a sequence are 6 12 20 30 42

a Work out the general term for this sequence.

> **Hint:** If in a sequence of numbers, the second differences are the same, then the nth term is of the form $an^2 + bn + c$, where a is half the value of the second difference. This is called a quadratic sequence. To find the rest of the nth term work out the difference between the original terms and an^2. The nth term for this new sequence will form the '$bn + c$' of the nth term for the quadratic sequence

b Work out the 19th term.

c One of the terms of this sequence is 1980, work out the position of this term.

9 Show that the equation $2x^{-2} + 3x = 25$ has a root between $x = 8$ and $x = 9$.

> **Hint:** A function $f(x) = 0$ has a solution between $x = a$ and $x = b$ if there is a change of sign between $f(a)$ and $f(b)$. This shows the graph of $f(x)$ crosses the x axis between these 2 values of x.

10 **a** Show that the equation $x^3 - 8x = 25$ has a root between $x = 3$ and $x = 4$.

_____

_____

b Show that the equation $x^3 - 8x = 25$ can be rearranged to give $x = \sqrt[3]{8x + 25}$.

_____

_____

c Use $x_{n+1} = \sqrt[3]{8x_n + 25}$ with $x_0 = 3.5$ to find a solution to the equation $x^3 - 8x = 25$ to 3 decimal places.

_____

_____

 11 Using $x_{n+1} = -4 - \dfrac{6}{x_n^2}$ with $x_0 = -4.5$

a Find the values of x_1, x_2, and x_3.

_____

_____

b Explain the connection between the values of x_1, x_2, and x_3 and identify the equation they relate to.

_____

_____

12 The first three terms of a Fibonacci sequence are $p, q, p + q$.

The third term is 9 and the fifth term is 23.

Find the values of p and q.

> **Hint:** A Fibonacci sequence is a sequence where the next term in the sequence is the sum of the two previous terms.

_____

_____

13 The first three terms of a Fibonacci sequence are $a, b, a + b$.

a Write down the next three terms of the sequence.

_____

b Show that the sum of the first six terms = $4 \times$ 5th term.

_____

_____

3 Ratio, proportion and change

3.1 Ratios, fractions and percentages

> **Hint:** $x : y = a : b$ can be written as $\dfrac{x}{y} = \dfrac{a}{b}$.

1 Work out the exact positive value of n such that:

a $n : 9 = 16 : n$

_____

b $n : 5 = 4 : n$

_____

2 Daichi and Eiji share a flat.

Daichi pays $\dfrac{4}{9}$ of the rent.

a Express the amount of rent Eiji pays, E, to the amount of rent Daichi pays, D, as a ratio in its simplest form.

_____

The ratio for the rent is changed to $D : E = 7 : 6$. The total rent is \$955.63.

b Work out:

  i the fraction of the total rent Eiji now pays

    _____

  ii the amount of rent Daichi now pays.

    _____

3 Three friends, Danilo, Gloria and Jacinta, each have a bank account.

Danilo has $\dfrac{5}{7}$ of the amount of money that Gloria has in her bank account.

Jacinta has $\dfrac{5}{6}$ of the amount of money that Danilo has in his bank account.

a Given that Danilo has £D in his bank account, Gloria has £G and Jacinta has £J, write down the amount of money they each have in their bank accounts in the ratio $D : G : J$.

_____

b Given that the total sum of money in the three bank accounts is €1940, calculate how much of this sum is in Gloria's bank account.

_____

_____

c Show that if the sum of the money in the three accounts was a multiple of €97, then each person would have a whole number of Euros in their account.

_____

_____

_____

4 The populations of four countries, A, B, C and D are in the ratio $21.2 : 35.1 : 33 : 26.2$.

a Write this ratio in its simplest form.

_____

b The population of country A is 35 million.

Calculate the total population of all four countries, giving your answer to 5 significant figures.

_____

c After 10 years, the population of C has risen by 0.9%.

Calculate the new population, giving your answer to 5 significant figures.

_____

5 The ratio $(x - y) : (x + 2y)$ is equivalent to $1 : p$.

Express y in terms of x and p.

_____

_____

_____

6 **a** Given that $x : y = 3 : 4$, write an equation for y in terms of x.

_____

_____

b The value of x is increased by 20%. Find the ratio $x : y$ after this increase.

_____

_____

7 a Given that $x : y = 6 : 5$, write an equation for y in terms of x.

_____

_____

b The value of y is decreased by 10%. Find the ratio $x : y$ after this increase.

_____

_____

8 In 2017, a house in London was valued at £2.3 million.

The value of the house had increased by 3.7% each year since 2007.

a Work out the value of the house in 2007.

_____

_____

_____

b Work out the percentage increase in the value of the house from 2007 to 2017.

_____

_____

_____

9 _Wheetycrackles_ come in various sizes: small (S), medium (M) and extra-large (XL).

The mass of the extra-large box is 1200 g.

The mass of the extra-large box is $\frac{3}{2}$ of the mass of the medium box.

The mass of the medium box is $\frac{8}{3}$ of the mass of the small box.

a Calculate the mass of the small box of _Wheetycrackles_.

_____

_____

_____

b The manufacturers introduce another size of *Wheetycrackles*: large (L). The mass of the large box is 1025 g. Write the ratio of the masses S : M : L : XL in its simplest form.

_____

_____

_____

10 Sally makes some dark chocolates and some milk chocolates.

Some of the chocolates have hard centres; the rest have soft centres.

The ratio of the number of:

- dark chocolates to milk chocolates is 4 : 5
- dark chocolates with hard centres to dark chocolates with soft centres is 3 : 7
- milk chocolates with hard centres to milk chocolates with soft centres is 3 : 5.

Work out what fraction of the chocolates have soft centres.

> Hint: This question can be solved using a 'tree diagram' approach.

_____

_____

_____

11 Suki has two savings accounts.

a She invests a sum of money in one account earning 5% compound interest per annum.

At the end of 6 years, there is £1608.11 in the account.

Work out her initial investment.

_____

_____

_____

b Suki invests £1750 in a different account that pays compound interest.

At the end of 9 years, there is £2385.07 in the account.

Calculate the interest rate on the account, giving your answer correct to 4 significant figures.

_____

_____

_____

12 Bradley sells 216 smoothie drinks in the ratio small : medium : large = 5 : 7 : 12.

The profit he makes for:

- one medium drink is 1.5 times the profit for one small drink
- one large drink is 2.5 times the profit for one small drink.

The total profit Bradley makes is £450.45. Work out the profit for one small smoothie drink.

_____

_____

_____

3.2 Direct and inverse proportion

Hint: $y \propto x$ means y is **directly** proportional to x. This can be written as $y = kx$, where k is the constant of proportionality. $y \propto \dfrac{1}{x}$ means y is **inversely** proportional to x. This can be written as $y = \dfrac{k}{x}$, where k is the constant of proportionality.

1 The graphs show different proportional relationships.

Label each graph with the proportional relationship it represents.

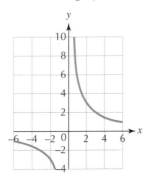 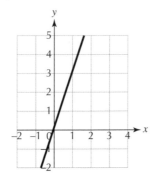 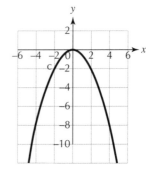

_____   _____   _____

2 y is directly proportional to x. When $x = 28$, $y = 7$.

   a Express y in terms of x.

_____

_____

   b Find x when $y = 3$. _____

   c Find y when $x = 44$. _____

3 y is inversely proportional to x. When $x = 20$, $y = 5$.

a Find x when $y = 10$.

_____

_____

b Find y when $x = 25$. _____

4 **a** A is directly proportional to the square of r.

When $r = 5$, $A = 78.5$, find:

i A when $r = 7$ _____

ii r when $A = 224$. _____

b The volume of a sphere is directly proportional to the cube of its radius.

When the radius of the sphere is 4 cm, its volume is $\frac{256}{3}\pi$ cm³.

Find the volume, in terms of π, of a sphere with radius 18 cm.

_____

_____

_____

_____

5 The cooking time in a microwave oven is inversely proportional to its power. The five power settings on a microwave oven are shown in the table below.

Level	Power (W)
Full	800
Heat	600
Simmer	350
Defrost	200
Warm	150

a A jacket potato takes 8 minutes on 'Full'. How long would it take on 'Heat'?

_____

b A large bowl of soup takes 12 minutes on 'Simmer'. How long will it take on 'Heat'?

_____

Hint: If y is proportional to x, this means that y is **directly** proportional to x.

6 Complete the missing value in each table and match each statement to a table.

a y is inversely proportional   Table ____
to x.

Table A

X	1	2	3
Y	0.5	2	

b y is directly proportional   Table ____
to x^2.

Table B

X	1	2	3
Y		2.5	1.66 (3 sf)

c y is inversely proportional   Table ____
to x^2.

Table C

X	1	2	3
Y	10		1.11 (2 dp)

7 The force of attraction, F, between two magnets is inversely proportional to the square of the distance, d, between them. When the magnets are 5 cm apart, the force of attraction is 22 newtons. How far apart are they when the force of attraction is 88 newtons?

_____

_____

_____

_____

8 a is inversely proportional to b. Complete the table.

a	2	4		10
b	4		8	

9 The number of days (d) it takes to build a wall is inversely proportional to the number of bricklayers (b) available.

It takes 8 bricklayers 12 days to build a wall.

Calculate:

a the number of days it would take 10 bricklayers to build the same size wall

_____

_____

b the number of bricklayers needed to build the same size wall in 3 days.

_____

_____

3.3 Compound measure

A compound measure is made up of two or more different measures. Examples of units include speed in km/h; acceleration in m/s²; density in g/cm³; pressure in N/cm².

You can use this triangle to remember the connection between distance, D, speed, S, and time T:

$$\text{speed} = \frac{\text{distance}}{\text{time}}$$

1   Calculate the time taken to travel:

     a   54 miles at an average speed of 90 mph, giving your answer in minutes

_____

     b   297 km at an average speed of 132 km/h, giving your answer in hours and minutes

_____

     c   10 metres at an average speed of 14 cm/s, giving your answer in seconds correct to 2 significant figures

_____

     d   162 km at an average speed of 37.5 m/s.

_____

2   Calculate the speed, in km/h, of particles travelling:

     a   117 m in 6.5 seconds

_____

     b   6700 m in 2 minutes

_____

     c 3×10^5 mm in 10 minutes

_____

     d 6×10^4 cm in 18 minutes.

_____

3   Calculate the distance covered when travelling at:

     a   83 km/h for 55 minutes, giving your answer to 2 significant figures

_____

     b   2560 km/h for 10 minutes, giving your answer to 3 significant figures

_____

c 12 m/s for 75 minutes, giving your answer in km

_____

d 5×10^3 m/s for 8×10^{-1} seconds, giving your answer in km.

_____

④ The average speed for a 4.5 hour car journey was 80 km/h.

In the final $\frac{3}{4}$ hour of the journey, the speed was 95 km/h.

Calculate:

a the distance travelled

_____

_____

b the speed for the first part of the journey.

_____

_____

> **Hint:** These are the kinematics formulae which involve using compound units for distance speed and time. They are also called suvat equations.
> Where:
> s is displacement from the position when $t = 0$
> u is initial velocity
> v is final velocity
> t is time taken
> $v = u + at$
> $s = ut + \frac{1}{2}ab\ at^2$
> $v^2 = u^2 + 2as$

⑤ A car starts from rest and travels with constant acceleration a m/s².

When $t = 6$ s, $v = 5$ m/s.

a Find the acceleration of the car.

> **Hint:** If a particle starts from rest then $u = 0$ when $t = 0$

_____

_____

b Find the displacement after 6 seconds.

_____

_____

_____

_____

6 The mass of 0.7 m³ of a metal alloy is 605 kg.

Calculate the density of this alloy, giving your answer in g/cm³.

> Hint: You can use this triangle to remember the connection between density, *D*, mass, *M*, and volume, *V*.
>
> density = $\dfrac{\text{mass}}{\text{volume}}$
>
>

_____

_____

7 A piece of plywood is made up of three layers of different woods, ash, cedar and hickory.

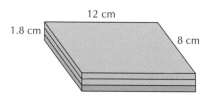

Each of the layers that make up the plywood has the same thickness.

The dimensions of the plywood are 12 cm by 8 cm by 1.8 cm.

The density of ash is 0.56 g/cm³, the density of hickory is 0.72 g/cm³ and the density of cedar is 0.35 g/cm³.

Calculate the mass of the plywood, giving your answer to 3 significant figures.

_____

_____

_____

8 Two cuboid ingots are made, one from tin and one from silver.

The cuboids are of equal mass but do not have the same dimensions.

The dimensions of the tin cuboid are 48 mm × 16mm × 20mm.

The dimensions of the silver cuboid are in direct proportion to the dimensions of the tin cuboid.

The density of tin is 7.3 g/cm³.

The density of silver is 10.49 g/cm³.

Calculate:

a the mass of the tin ingot

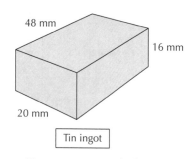

Diagram **not** accurately drawn

_____

_____

b the dimensions of the silver ingot, giving your answers to 3 significant figures.

_____

_____

9   A pin has a force of 90 N acting on it.

Force = 90 N

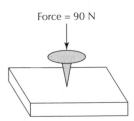

Hint: You can use this triangle to remember the connection between pressure, *P*, force, *F*, and area *A*.

$$\text{pressure} = \frac{\text{force}}{\text{area}}$$

Calculate:

a   the pressure if the area of the top of the pin is 2.8×10^{-7} m²

_____

_____

b   the area of the top of the pin if the pressure exerted is 5×10^{7} N/m².

_____

_____

10   The diagram shows a system of pistons A and B.

A force of 17 N pushes down on hydraulic oil in piston A.

This causes the hydraulic oil to push upwards in piston B.

The force in piston A exerts pressure on an area of 20 cm².

The hydraulic oil pushes up on an area of 45 cm² in piston B.

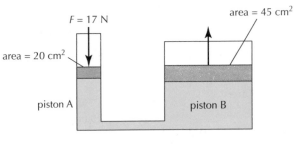

Hydraulic oil

Calculate the force exerted by the hydraulic oil on piston B.

_____

_____

_____

_____

_____

11 A particle starts with initial velocity u m/s and travels with constant acceleration 2 m/s².

a Find s m in terms of u when $v = 2u$.

> Hint: You will need to use the kinematics formulae from Question 5.

_____

_____

b When $s = 10$ m, the ratio of $u : v$ is $3 : 5$. Find the exact value of u.

12 Bronze is an alloy of copper and tin with mass in the ratio $C : T = 22 : 3$.
The density of tin is 7.31 g/cm³ and the density of copper is 8.92 g/cm³.

a Calculate the mass of tin needed to make a bronze bowl with a total mass of 1.7 kg.

_____

_____

_____

b A bronze plaque is made with 250 g of copper.

i Calculate the total mass of the plaque.

_____

_____

_____

ii Calculate the mass of 1 cm³ of bronze.

_____

_____

_____

3.4 Ratios of length, area and volume

1 The points P, Q, R and S lie in order on a straight line.

PQ : PS = 1 : 9

QR : QS = 7 : 16

Work out PQ : QR : RS.

_____

_____

2 Two identical triangles overlap as shown by the shaded area.

The shaded area is 25% of each triangle.

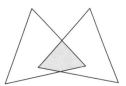

Calculate the percentage of the combined shape which is not shaded, giving your answer correct to 3 significant figures.

_____

_____

3 A and B are two rectangles.

Rectangle A has width $3b$ and height h.

Rectangle B has width b and height $2h$.

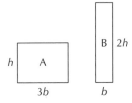

Given that the perimeter of rectangle A is equal to the perimeter of rectangle B, work out the ratio $h : b$.

_____

_____

_____

4 P and Q are two cuboids.

Cuboid P has width $3z$, height y and depth $2x$ and cuboid Q has width x, height $2y$ and depth $3z$.

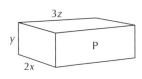

a Calculate the ratio of the volume of cuboid P to cuboid Q.

_____

_____

b Prove that the volume of cuboid Q is always double that of cuboid P.

_____

_____

_____

_____

_____

5 A, B and C are three similar rectangles.

The ratio of the area of rectangles A, B and C is $2 : 3 : 5$.

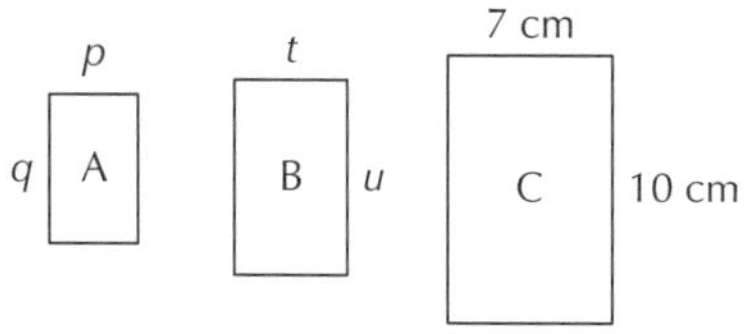

a Calculate the area of:

   i   rectangle A

_____

   ii rectangle B.

_____

b Calculate, in surd form, the length of the base and the length of the height of:

   i   rectangle A

_____

_____

   ii rectangle B.

_____

_____

6 A and B are similar triangles.

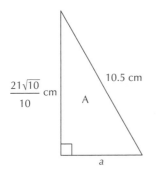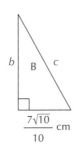

Diagrams **not** accurately drawn

Work out the exact values of the lengths of the following sides.

a Side *a* _____

b Side *b* _____

c Side *c* _____

 7 A graphic designer designs a new logo for a fishmonger's shop.

The logo for the shop front will be made in the ratio 6.5 : 1 of the original paper design.

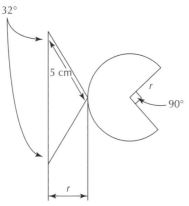

Diagram **not** accurately drawn

a Calculate the area of the triangular tail of the fish that will be on the logo for the shop front.

> **Hint:** The area of a triangle ABC can be found using area $= \frac{1}{2}ab \sin C$.

_____

b Work out the ratio of the area of the fish tail to the area of the head on the fish logo in its simplest form. Give your answers for the individual areas on the logo correct to 3 significant figures.

_____

_____

_____

8 The ratio of the lengths of the sides of two cubes A and B is $a : b$.

a State the ratio of:

   i the surface areas of A and B

_____

   ii the volumes of A and B.

_____

The lengths of the sides of cube A are increased by 8%.

The lengths of the sides of cube B are decreased by 10%.

b Find the new ratios, in terms of a and b in their simplest form, for:

   i the lengths of the sides of A and B

_____

_____

   ii the surface areas of A and B

_____

_____

   iii the volumes of A and B.

_____

_____

4 Geometry and measures

4.1 Arcs and sectors 🖩

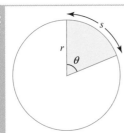

The yellow area is called a **sector** of a circle; the curved edge of the sector, s, is called an **arc**. As the angle at the centre, θ, is less than 180°, the diagram shows a minor sector and a minor arc. (If greater than 180°, they would be a major sector and major arc.)

For a sector of a circle radius r, with angle at centre θ,

arc length $= 2\pi r \times \dfrac{\theta}{360}$; area of sector $= \pi r^2 \times \dfrac{\theta}{360}$.

---

1 Calculate the arc length of these sectors, giving your answers correct to 3 significant figures.

a

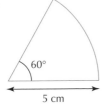

60°

5 cm

b

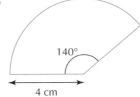

140°

4 cm

c

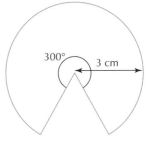

300°   3 cm

_____

_____

_____

---

2 Calculate the area of these sectors, giving your answers in terms of π.

a

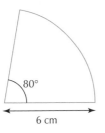

80°

6 cm

b

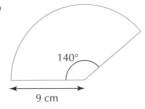

140°

9 cm

c

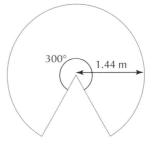

300°   1.44 m

_____

_____

_____

3 Calculate the angle, θ, at the centre of these sectors.

a

π cm
θ
3 cm

_____

_____

_____

b

$\frac{\pi}{3}$ cm
θ
5 cm

_____

_____

_____

c

$\frac{7\pi}{9}$ cm
θ
7 cm

_____

_____

_____

4 Carly plans to lay a patio in the corner of her garden.

a What is the area of the patio? Give your answer correct to 2 decimal places.

_____

_____

_____

65°
4.5 m

Carly wants to add an edging of bricks to the curved edge of the patio. Each brick is 20 cm long.

b How many bricks does she need for the edging?

_____

_____

_____

Diagram **not** accurately drawn

5 The area of this sector is $\frac{605}{48}\pi$ cm².

Calculate the angle at the centre for a sector from the same circle with an area of $\frac{2057}{576}\pi$.

150°

> **Hint:** Remember to check that your calculator is in degrees mode.

_____

_____

_____

_____

6 The diagram shows an equilateral triangle PQR with sides of length 8 cm.

A is the midpoint of PQ.

B is the midpoint of AR.

PAB is a sector of a circle, centre P.

Calculate the area of the shaded region.

Give your answer correct to 3 significant figures.

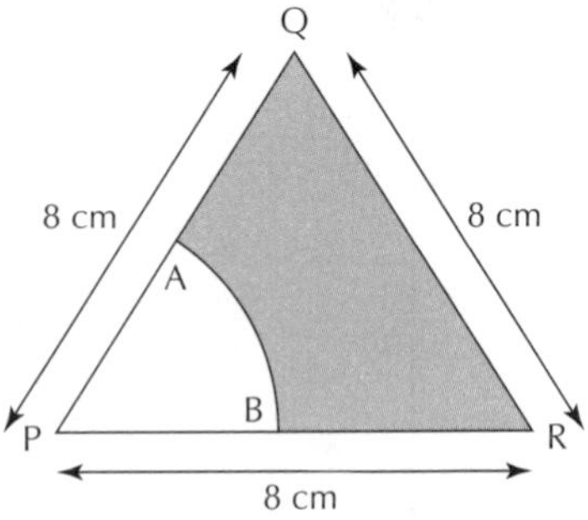

Diagram **not** accurately drawn

_____

_____

_____

_____

7

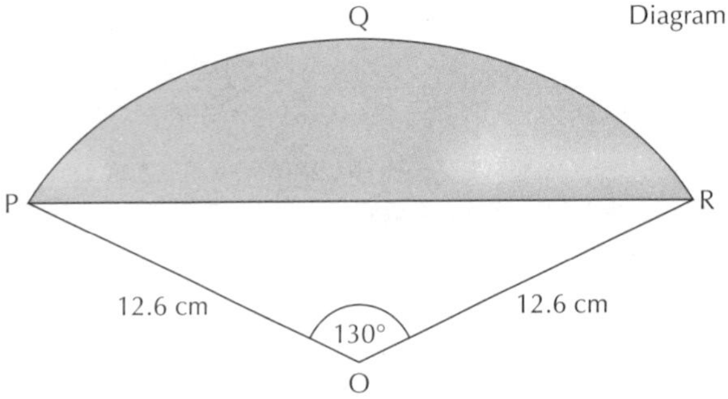

Diagram **not** accurately drawn

The diagram shows a sector OPQR of a circle with centre O.

OP = OQ = 12.6 cm

Angle POQ = 130°.

Calculate the area of the shaded segment POQ.

Give your answer correct to 3 significant figures.

Hint: Area of a segment = area of sector – area of triangle

_____

_____

_____

_____

_____

_____

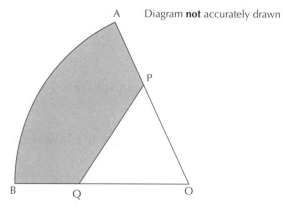

Diagram **not** accurately drawn

OAB is a sector of a circle with centre O and radius 12 cm.

P is the point on OA and Q is the point on OB such that OP : OA = OQ : OB = 2 : 3 and OPQ is an equilateral triangle.

Calculate the area of the shaded region as a percentage of the area of the sector OAB.

Give your answer correct to 1 decimal place.

_____

_____

_____

_____

_____

9

OPR is a sector of a circle centre O, radius 10 m.

PQ is the tangent to the circle at point P.

RQ is the tangent to the circle at point R.

Angle POR = 130°.

Calculate the area of the shaded region.

Give your answer correct to 3 significant figures.

> Hint: Angle between radius and tangent is 90°.

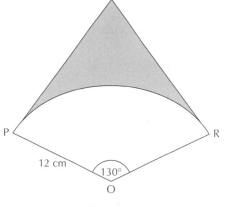

Diagram **not** accurately drawn

_____

_____

_____

_____

_____

_____

4.2 Surface area and volume 🖩

Surface area of cylinder = $2\pi rh + 2\pi r^2$; surface area of cone = $\pi r^2 + \pi rl$; surface area of sphere = $4\pi r^2$.

Volume of cylinder = $\pi r^2 h$; volume of cone = $\frac{1}{3}\pi r^2 h$; volume of sphere = $\frac{4}{3}\pi r^3$.

1 A hemisphere fits exactly on top of a solid cylinder of height 10 cm, as shown in the diagram.

The volume of the cylinder is 129.6π cm³. Calculate the total surface area of the 3D object.

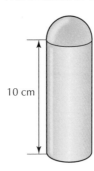

Diagram **not** accurately drawn

10 cm

_____

_____

_____

_____

_____

2 Calculate the difference in the surface areas of the cylinder and cone.

Diagram **not** accurately drawn

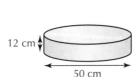

12 cm

50 cm

30 cm

30 cm

_____

_____

_____

_____

_____

_____

_____

3 The 3D shape in the diagram is made up of a cylinder and a cone.

Find the volume of the shape, giving your answer in terms of π.

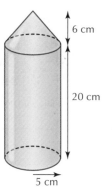

Diagram **not** accurately drawn

6 cm

20 cm

5 cm

_____

_____

_____

_____

_____

4 The 3D shape in the diagram is made from a cylinder
and a hemisphere.

Find the total surface area of the shape, giving your answer in terms of π.

20 cm

5 cm
Diagram **not**
accurately drawn

_____

_____

_____

_____

_____

5 Three spheres of radius 3 cm can just fit into a closed cylinder.

What is the volume of empty space in the cylinder? Give your answer to
the nearest cm³.

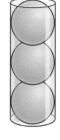

_____

_____

_____

_____

6 A wooden cone of perpendicular height 15 cm and base radius 12 cm has the top 5 cm in height removed to leave a frustum. The wood has a density of 0.78 g/cm³.

Find, to the nearest gram, the mass of the frustum.

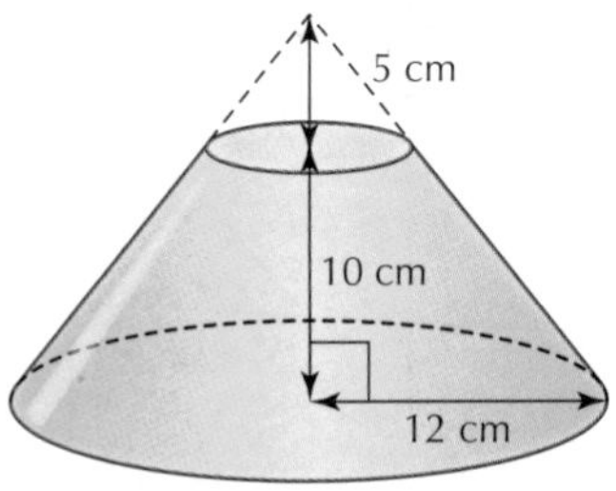

_____

_____

_____

_____

Diagram **not** accurately drawn

7 **a** An artist makes a concrete statue which is made up of a cylinder with a right circular cone on top, as shown in the diagram. The concrete has a density of 2.4 g/cm³.

What is the mass of the statue, to the nearest kilogram?

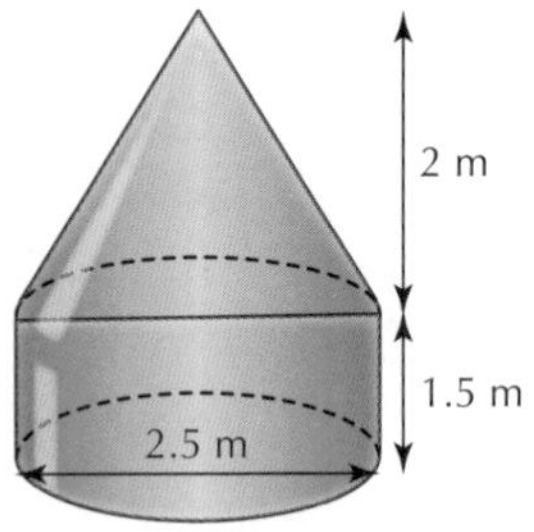

_____

_____

_____

_____

Diagram **not** accurately drawn

b The artist plans to cover the total outer surface of his statue with gold leaf. Gold leaf is sold in books of 25 sheets. One book of gold leaf sheets costs £18.95. Each sheet measures 80 mm by 80 mm.

How much will it cost to cover the total outer surface of the statue with a single layer of gold leaf?

_____

_____

_____

8 The diagram shows the cross section of a 3D object made up of a hemisphere and a cone.

Calculate the volume of the object.

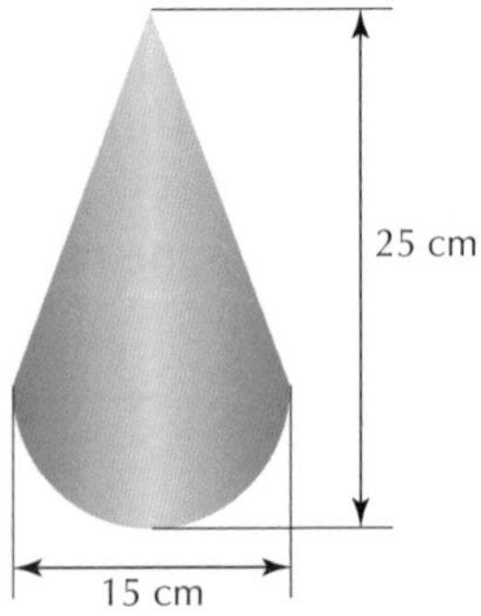

_____

_____

_____

_____

_____

Diagram **not** accurately drawn

1 In the diagram, AOD and BOC are straight lines.

CD is parallel to AB.

CD = 15 cm, AB = 25 cm.

The total height of the two triangles is 50 cm.

Calculate the height, h, of triangle AOB.

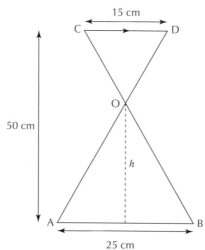

15 cm   Diagram **not** accurately drawn

50 cm

h

25 cm

_____

_____

_____

2 Two prisms *A* and *B* are mathematically similar.

The area of the front face of the large prism is 220 cm².

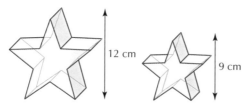

Diagram **not** accurately drawn

12 cm   9 cm

a Calculate the area of the front face of the small prism.

_____

_____

b The prisms are made from the same type of glass. The mass of the small prism is 225 g. Calculate the mass of the large prism.

_____

_____

_____

3 Two cuboids P and Q are mathematically similar.

Their surface areas are 628 cm² and 12 717 cm², respectively. The volume of the smaller cuboid is 1040 cm³.

Find the volume of the larger cuboid.

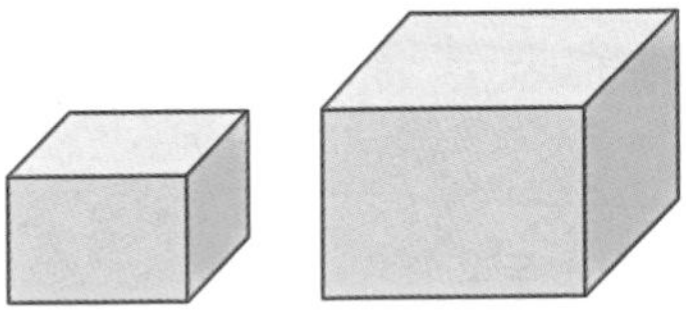

Diagram **not** accurately drawn

_____

_____

_____

4 Ronson has been asked to draw a scale drawing of this right-angled triangle.

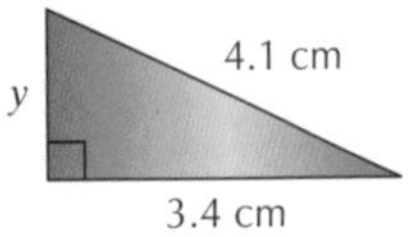

4.1 cm   Diagram **not** accurately drawn

y

3.4 cm

a The scale factor for the scale drawing is $\frac{4}{3}$.

Calculate the vertical height of the triangle on the scale drawing.

_____

_____

_____

b Calculate the area of the triangle in the scale drawing.

_____

_____

_____

5 The diagram shows two right-angled triangles, ABC and ADE. The length $AB = \frac{7}{4}AD$.

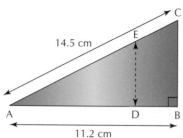

Diagram **not** accurately drawn

Calculate the length of DE.

_____

_____

6 The area of triangle A, shown in the diagram, is $12\sqrt{2}$ cm².

a Calculate the value of x and hence find the perimeter of the triangle.

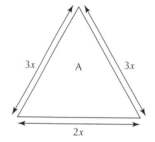

_____

_____

_____

_____

b Triangle B is similar to triangle A.

The area of triangle B is $24\sqrt{2}$ cm².

Calculate the perimeter of triangle B.

_____

_____

_____

7 A and B are two geometrically similar solid shapes.

The total surface area of shape A is 540 cm².

The total surface area of shape B is 1500 cm².

The volume of shape A is 2430 cm³.

Calculate the volume of shape B.

_____

_____

_____

8

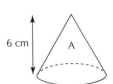

6 cm

Two cones, A and B, are mathematically similar.

The total surface area of cone A is 96 cm².

The total surface area of cone B is 216 cm².

The height of cone A is 6 cm.

a Work out the height of cone B.

_____

_____

The volume of cone A is 24 cm³.

b Work out the volume of cone B.

_____

_____

 9 Two cylinders, A and B, are mathematically similar.

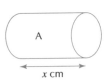
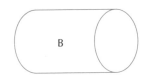

Diagram **not** accurately drawn

x cm

The volume of cylinder A is 243π cm³.

The volume of cylinder B is 1125π cm³.

The total length of cylinder A and cylinder B is 24 cm.

a Find the length, x cm, of cylinder A.

_____

_____

_____

_____

The total surface area of cylinder A and cylinder B is 1020π cm².

b Work out the surface area of cylinder B. Give your answer as a multiple of π.

_____

_____

_____

10 The diagram shows a frustrum.

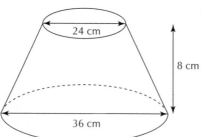

Diagram **not** accurately drawn

24 cm

8 cm

36 cm

Calculate the volume of the frustrum. Give your answer in terms of π.

_____

_____

_____

_____

11 The two triangles in the diagram are similar.

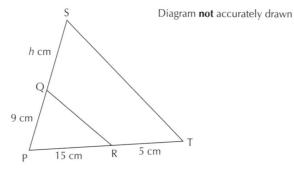

Diagram **not** accurately drawn

S

h cm

Q

9 cm

P   15 cm   R   5 cm   T

There are two possible values of *h*.

Work out each of these values in exact form.

State any assumptions you make in your working.

_____

_____

_____

_____

_____

_____

_____

4.4 Trigonometry 🖩

> **Hint:** To solve problems involving sides and angles of right-angled triangles, use either **Pythagoras' theorem:** in any right-angled triangle ABC, $a^2 = b^2 + c^2$, where a is the length of the hypotenuse (the hypotenuse is the longest side) or **SOHCAHTOA:**
>
>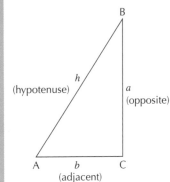
>
> $$\text{SOHCAHTOA: } \sin = \frac{\text{opp}}{\text{hyp}},$$
>
> $$\cos = \frac{\text{adj}}{\text{hyp}},$$
>
> $$\tan = \frac{\text{opp}}{\text{adj}}$$
>
> Remember to check that your calculator is in degrees mode.

1 An aeroplane is flying at a constant height of 10 000 m. An observer in the plane measures the angle of depression to a point on the ground as 30°. Twenty seconds later, the angle of depression to the same point on the ground is 35°.

a Work out the horizontal distance travelled by the plane in 20 seconds.

_____

_____

_____

_____

b What is the speed of the plane, in km/h?

_____

_____

2 The diagram shows a quadrilateral PQRS.

PQ = 18 cm, PS = 14 cm.

Angle QRS = 50°;
angle PSR = angle RQS = 90°.

Calculate the length of RS.
Give your answer correct to
3 significant figures.

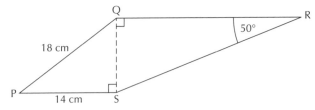

Diagram **not** accurately drawn

_____

_____

_____

3 PQR is a triangle.

PSR is a straight line with QS perpendicular to PR.

PQ = 9 cm, QR = 15 cm.

Angle QPS = 70°.

Calculate the length of PR. Give your answer correct to 3 significant figures.

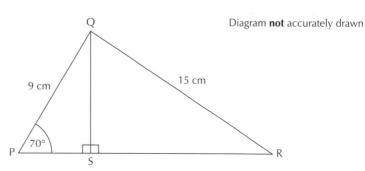

Diagram **not** accurately drawn

_____

_____

_____

4 Without using a calculator, use the triangles shown to complete the table with the exact values of the trigonometric ratios.

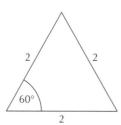 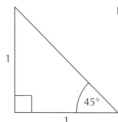

Diagram **not** accurately drawn

	sin	cos	tan
30°			
45°			
60°			
90°			

5 The diagram shows a cuboid.

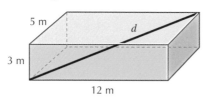

Diagram **not** accurately drawn

Work out the angle that the diagonal, d, makes with the base of the cuboid.

_____

_____

_____

6 The diagram shows a triangular prism.

AB = 10 cm, BD = 3 cm and DF = 9 cm.

a Find the length of EB.

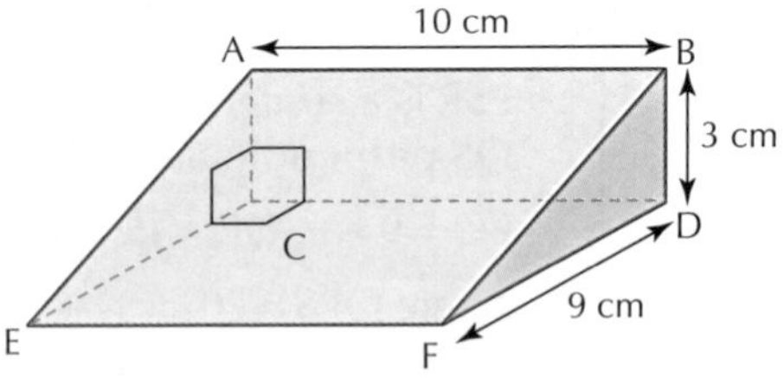

_____

_____

_____

_____

b Find the size of angle BFD.

_____

_____

c Find the size of angle AFC.

_____

_____

10 cm

A ←——————→ B

3 cm

C

D

9 cm

E

F

Diagram **not** accurately drawn

7 Rajesh stands near an office block and measures the angle of elevation to the top of the building as 68°. He then moves 50 m further away and measures the angle of elevation as 43°.

How tall is the office block?

Hint: Use the tan function for the two right-angled triangles to find an expression for the height and solve simultaneously.

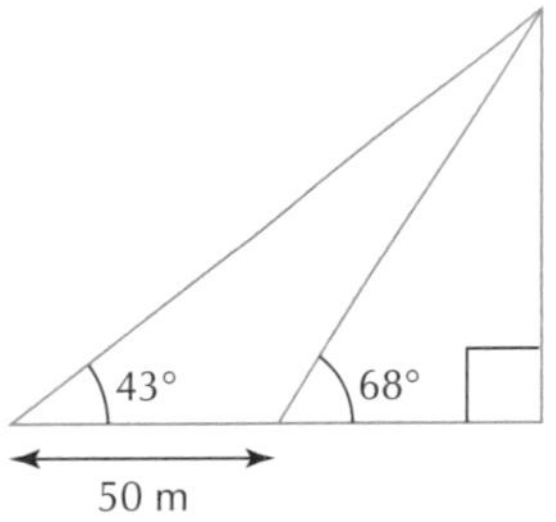

Diagram **not** accurately drawn

43°   68°

50 m

_____

_____

_____

_____

_____

_____

8 The diagram shows a rectangular-based pyramid.

V is vertically above the centre of the rectangle.

$AB = CD = 10$ cm, $AD = BC = 12$ cm.

$AV = BV = CV = DV = 20$ cm.

Calculate the angle that AV makes with the base ABCD.

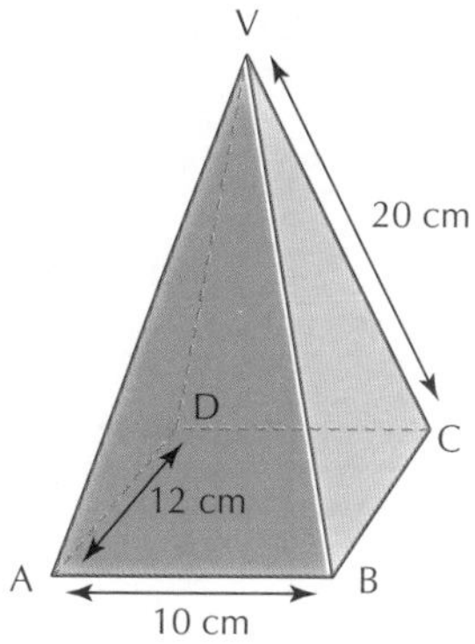

Diagram **not** accurately drawn

_____

_____

_____

_____

_____

_____

_____

_____

_____

9 A straight thin rod of length 30 cm is placed inside a cylindrical container with height 32 cm and circumference $5\sqrt{11}\pi$ cm. The bottom of the rod rests at a point where the base meets the side of the cylinder and the top of the rod rests against the side of the cylinder.

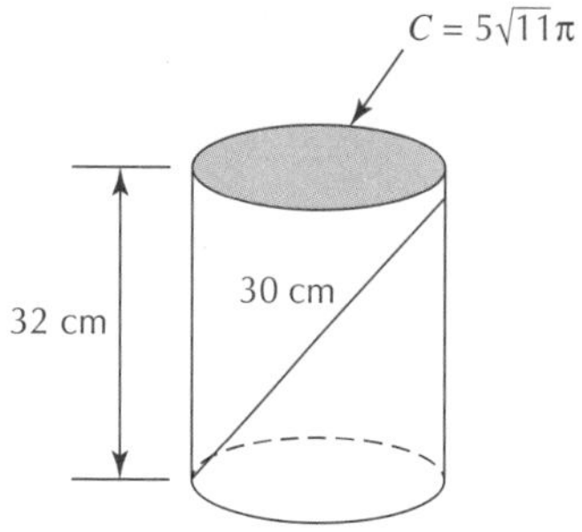

Diagram **not** accurately drawn

a Calculate the distance from the top of the cylinder to the top end of the rod.

_____

_____

_____

b Calculate the angle that the rod makes with the base of the cylinder.

_____

_____

_____

_____

10 In the diagram, the hypotenuse of the right-angled triangle is of length $\frac{2\sqrt{5}}{3}$ cm and its height is $\frac{\sqrt{15}}{3}$ cm. Without the use of a calculator, show that angle θ is 60°. You must show your working.

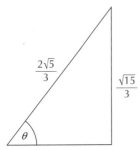

_____

_____

_____

_____

_____

4.5 Sine rule and cosine rule

Hint: Sine rule: $\dfrac{a}{\sin A} = \dfrac{b}{\sin B} = \dfrac{c}{\sin C}$

Cosine rule: $a^2 = b^2 + c^2 - 2bc \cos A$

Use the cosine rule if you have all three sides, or two sides and the included angle; in all other cases, use the sine rule.

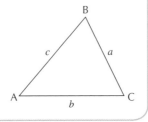

1 Calculate the value of x in each of these triangles.

a

Diagrams **not** accurately drawn

b

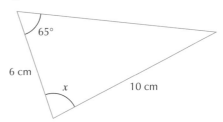

_____   _____

_____   _____

_____   _____

2 Two ships leave port at the same time. Ship A travels at a constant speed of 14 km/h on a bearing of 065°. Ship B travels at a constant speed of 21 km/h on a bearing of 135°. Calculate the distance between ships A and B after one hour.

N

14 km

Port

A

21 km

B

Diagram **not** accurately drawn

_____

_____

_____

_____

_____

_____

3 The lengths of the adjacent sides of a parallelogram are 10 cm and 15 cm. The length of the longer diagonal is 19 cm. Work out the length of the shorter diagonal.

Hint: Draw a sketch and use the properties of a parallelogram.

_____

_____

_____

_____

_____

_____

4 A boat sails from port 20 km due east to a lighthouse. It then changes course and sails 50 km on a bearing of 150° to a buoy. The boat then sails directly back to port.

a How far does the boat sail in total?

_____

_____

_____

_____

b On what bearing does the boat sail back from the buoy to the port?

_____

_____

_____

_____

4.6 Areas of triangles ▦

> **Hint:** Area of triangle $= \frac{1}{2} ab \sin C$

1   Calculate the area of the isosceles triangle.

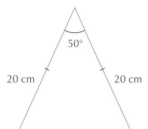

Diagram **not** accurately drawn

50°

20 cm   20 cm

_____

_____

_____

_____

2   Find the area of this triangular field. Give your answer correct to 3 significant figures.

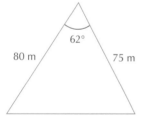

Diagram **not** accurately drawn

62°

80 m   75 m

_____

_____

3   A farmer estimates the area of this field as 34 500 m².

Find the difference between the actual area of the triangular
field and the farmer's estimate.

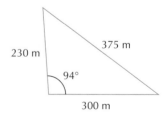

230 m   375 m

94°

300 m

Diagram **not**
accurately drawn

_____

_____

_____

_____

_____

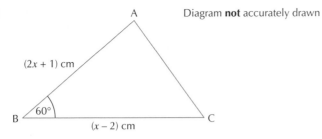

Diagram **not** accurately drawn

(2x + 1) cm

60°

B

(x − 2) cm

C

A

The area of triangle ABC is $5\sqrt{3}$ cm².

Calculate the value of x. Give your answer correct to 3 significant figures.

_____

_____

_____

_____

5 Calculate the area of the field ABCD.

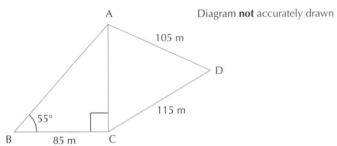

A

105 m

Diagram **not** accurately drawn

D

55°

115 m

B

85 m

C

_____

_____

_____

_____

_____

_____

_____

_____

_____

_____

_____

6 Work out the area of PQRS. Give your answer correct to 2 significant figures.

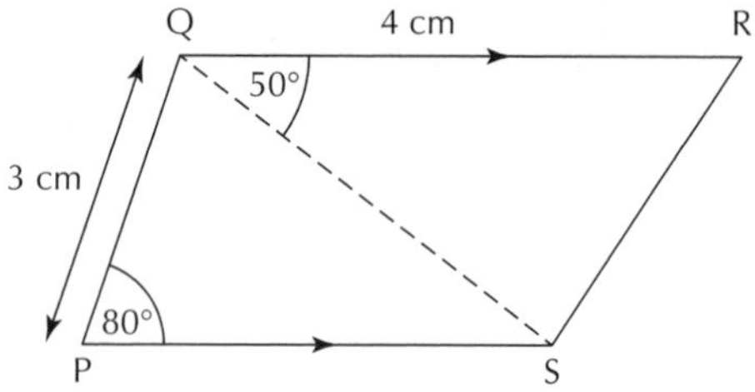

Diagram **not** accurately drawn

_____

_____

_____

_____

_____

_____

_____

_____

7 Farmer Smith has a triangular field, ABC. Farmer Jones has a field in the shape of a pentagon ACOPQ. The two fields share a border, AC. Farmer Jones says he will sell part of his field, triangle ACO, to Farmer Smith. QAB is a straight line pointing east. The line CO points due north.

Diagram **not** accurately drawn

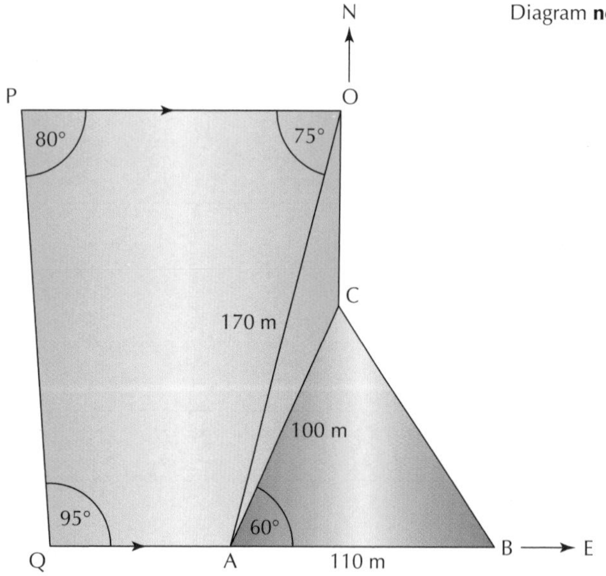

a Calculate the area of Farmer Smith's triangular field ABC.

_____

_____

_____

b Calculate the percentage increase in Farmer's Smith's field when he buys the extra field from Farmer Jones.

_____

_____

_____

_____

_____

_____

_____

_____

_____

4.7 Congruent triangles

> **Hint:** The rules for proving congruency are:
>
> SSS all three sides equal
>
> SAS two sides and the included angle are equal
>
> AAS two angles and a corresponding side are equal
>
> RHS right angle, hypotenuse and one other side are equal.

1 ABCD is a parallelogram.

Prove that triangle ABC is congruent to triangle CDA.

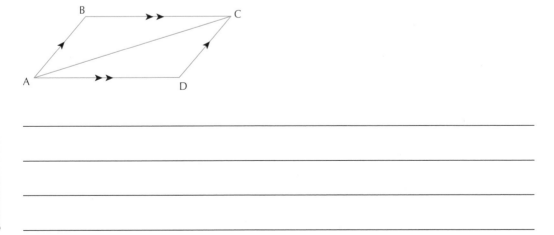

_____

_____

_____

_____

2 In the diagram, AB is equal in length and parallel to DE.

Prove that triangle ABC is congruent to triangle EDC.

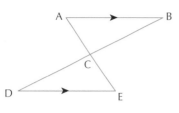

_____

_____

_____

_____

3 ABCD is a quadrilateral with AB = AD and BC = CD.

Prove that angle ABC = angle ADC.

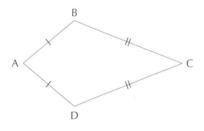

_____

_____

_____

_____

4 ABCDE is a regular pentagon.

Prove that triangle ABC is congruent to triangle CDE.

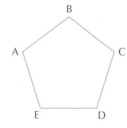

_____

_____

_____

_____

5 ABCDEF is a regular hexagon with sides of length 10 cm.

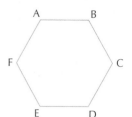

a Show that the area of the hexagon is $150\sqrt{3}$ cm².

_____

_____

_____

b Use your results from part **a** to prove that the area of any regular hexagon with sides of length x is $\frac{3\sqrt{3}}{2}x^2$.

_____

_____

_____

_____

6 A regular octagon has sides of length 10 cm.

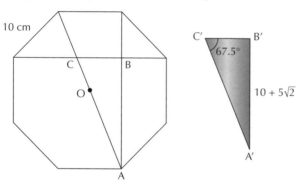

a Prove that triangle ABC is congruent to triangle A'B'C'.

_____

_____

_____

_____

_____

b Prove that the area of triangle ABC is P cm², where $60 < P < 61$.

_____

_____

_____

_____

1 Work out the size of the angles labelled *a* to *n*. Give reasons for your answers.

a

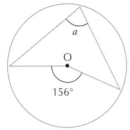

b

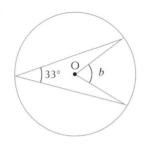

c

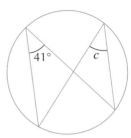

_____
_____

_____
_____

_____
_____

d

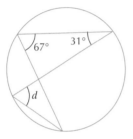

e

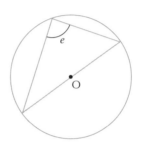

f

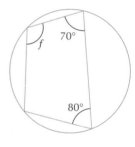

_____
_____

_____
_____

_____
_____

g

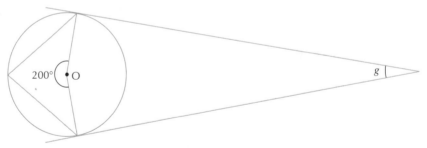

_____
_____

h

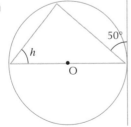

_____
_____

i

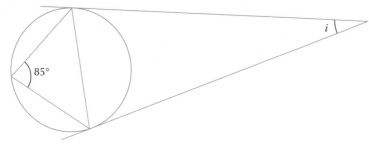

_____

_____

j

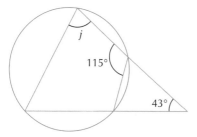

k

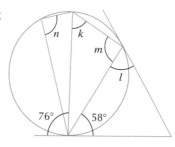

_____   _____

_____   _____

_____   _____

_____   _____

_____   _____

2 Prove that the angle in a semicircle is a right angle.

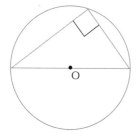

_____

_____

_____

_____

3 Prove that the angles marked θ in the diagram are equal.

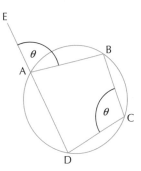

_____

_____

_____

_____

_____

_____

4 ABC is a tangent to the circle, centre O, at the point B.

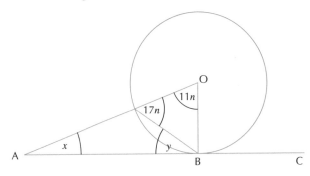

Calculate:

a angle x

_____

_____

_____

b angle y.

_____

_____

_____

5 Prove that the angles subtended at the circumference by the same arc in the same segment are equal.

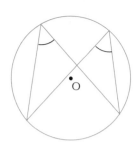

_____

_____

_____

_____

_____

6 Prove that the angle subtended by an arc at the centre of a circle is twice the angle subtended by the arc at the circumference.

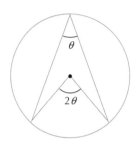

_____

_____

_____

_____

4.9 Enlargement

1 On the grid below, draw the enlargement of triangle A:

a by scale factor −1, centre (2, 0); label the image B

b by scale factor −2, centre (0, 0); label the image C

c by scale factor $-\frac{1}{2}$, centre (−5, 3); label the image D.

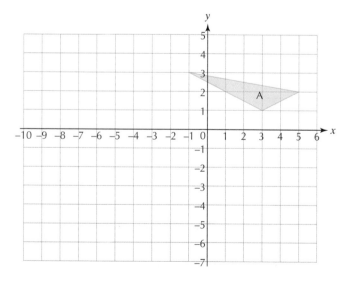

2 Triangle ABC has been enlarged to give triangle A'B'C'.

  a Write down the scale factor of the enlargement.

  _____

  _____

  b Draw construction lines to identify the position of the centre of enlargement.

  c Write down the coordinates of the centre of enlargement.

  _____

  _____

  d Describe the inverse transformation that would take A'B'C' back to ABC.

  _____

  _____

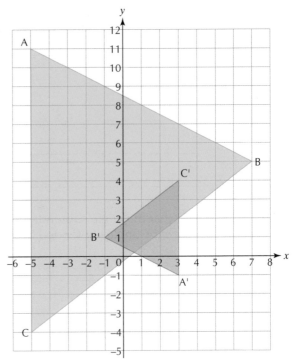

3 A small square (A) and a triangle (B) are enlarged from different centres to form shape C.

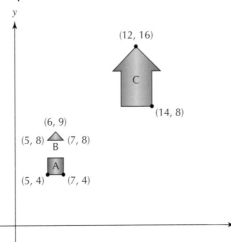

  a What is the scale factor of the enlargement that maps B onto C?

  _____

  _____

  b What are the scale factor and centre of the enlargement that maps A onto C?

  _____

  _____

4.10 Vectors

1 In the parallelogram grid, $\overrightarrow{OA} = \mathbf{a}$ and $\overrightarrow{OB} = \mathbf{b}$.

a Name two vectors equivalent to **a**. _____ _____

b Name two vectors equivalent to **b**. _____ _____

c Name two vectors equivalent to −**a**. _____ _____

d Name two vectors equivalent to −**b**. _____ _____

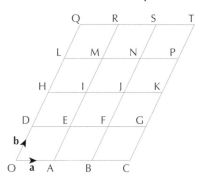

Write the following vectors in terms of **a** and **b**.

e $\overrightarrow{OC}$ = _____ **f** $\overrightarrow{FH}$ = _____ **g** $\overrightarrow{OT}$ = _____

h $\overrightarrow{AN}$ = _____ **i** $\overrightarrow{IK}$ = _____ **j** $\overrightarrow{NC}$ = _____

2 Identify and label the points C to J on the grid below.

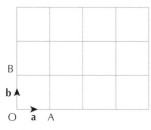

a $\overrightarrow{OC} = 3\mathbf{a}$ **b** $\overrightarrow{OD} = 2\mathbf{b}$ **c** $\overrightarrow{OE} = 3\mathbf{a} + \mathbf{b}$ **d** $\overrightarrow{OF} = 2\mathbf{a} + 3\mathbf{b}$

e $\overrightarrow{OG} = 4\mathbf{a} + \frac{3}{2}\mathbf{b}$ **f** $\overrightarrow{OH} = \frac{5}{2}(\mathbf{a} + \mathbf{b})$ **g** $\overrightarrow{IO} = -3\mathbf{a} - 2\mathbf{b}$ **h** $\overrightarrow{JO} = -\frac{3}{2}\mathbf{a} - \frac{5}{2}\mathbf{b}$

3 $\overrightarrow{OA} = \mathbf{a}$, $\overrightarrow{OB} = \mathbf{b}$ and M is the midpoint of AB.
Write the following vectors in terms of **a** and **b**.

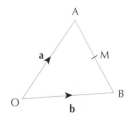

a $\overrightarrow{AB}$ = _____ **b** $\overrightarrow{AM}$ = _____

c $\overrightarrow{BA}$ = _____ **e** $\overrightarrow{BM}$ = _____

f $\overrightarrow{OM}$ = _____ **g** $\overrightarrow{MO}$ = _____

4 The diagram shows a regular hexagon ABCDEF with centre O.

Write the following vectors in terms of **a** and/or **b**.

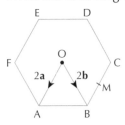

a $\overrightarrow{AB}$ = _____ **b** $\overrightarrow{DC}$ = _____ **c** $\overrightarrow{FE}$ = _____

M is the midpoint of BC.

d $\overrightarrow{EM}$ = _____

5 OAB is a triangle where $\overrightarrow{OA}$ = **a** and $\overrightarrow{OB}$ = **b**.

The point C is on AB such that AC : CB = 3 : 2.

$\overrightarrow{DC}$ is parallel to $\overrightarrow{OA}$.

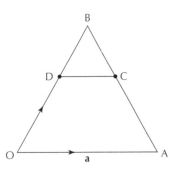

a Write $\overrightarrow{OC}$ in terms of **a** and **b** _____

b Write $\overrightarrow{DC}$ in terms of **a** _____

6 ABCD is a parallelogram where $\overrightarrow{AB}$ = **a** and $\overrightarrow{BC}$ = **b**.

Prove that vectors $\overrightarrow{BD}$ and $\overrightarrow{AC}$ bisect each other at m.

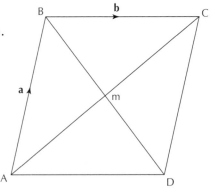

_____

_____

_____

_____

_____

_____

7 ABCD is a quadrilateral.

P is the midpoint of AB.

Q is the midpoint of BC.

R is the midpoint of CD.

S is the midpoint of AD.

Prove that PQRS is a parallelogram.

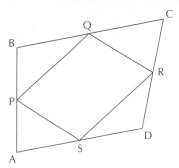

_____

_____

_____

_____

8

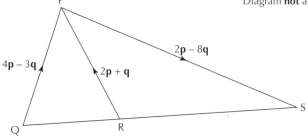

Diagram **not** accurately drawn

Is QRS a straight line?

Show working to support your answer.

_____

_____

_____

_____

9 OABC is a parallelogram.

$\overrightarrow{OA} = \mathbf{a}$ and $\overrightarrow{OC} = \mathbf{c}$.

P is the midpoint of the line AC.

OCD is a straight line such that OC : OD = 1 : k.

Given that $\overrightarrow{PD} = 4\mathbf{c} - \frac{1}{2}\mathbf{a}$, find k.

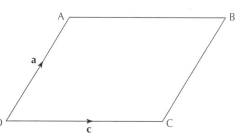

_____

_____

_____

_____

5 Statistics and probability

5.1 Cumulative frequency graphs and box plots

1 The table shows information about the length of time a sample of 100 people spent waiting to see their doctor at medical practice A.

Time, t (mins)	$0 \leqslant t < 5$	$5 \leqslant t < 10$	$10 \leqslant t < 15$	$15 \leqslant t < 20$	$20 \leqslant t < 25$	$25 \leqslant t < 30$
Frequency	18	7	35	22	11	7

a Draw a cumulative frequency graph to illustrate this data.

Hint: Cumulative frequency is plotted against the upper class boundary for each class interval.

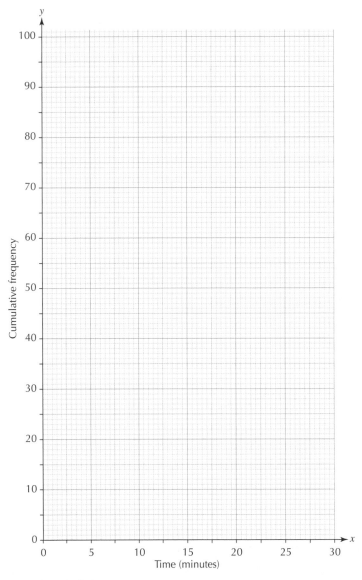

Hint: Draw appropriate lines on your graph to help you answer these questions. Use a ruler to make sure you are accurate.

b Use your cumulative frequency graph to estimate the following.

   i   The median waiting time _____

   ii The lower quartile _____

  iii The upper quartile _____

  iv The interquartile range _____

c How many people waited for up to 12 minutes? _____

d How many people waited for more than 22 minutes? _____

e How many people waited between 14 and 24 minutes? _____

The box plot shows information about the length of time a sample of 100 people spent waiting to see their doctor in medical practice B.

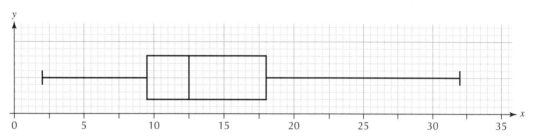

f Compare the distribution of waiting times for medical practice A with the distribution of waiting times for medical practice B.

Hint: Use a measure of spread and a measure of average to compare the distributions in context.

_____

_____

_____

g Comment on the statement: 'The range for medical practice A is the same as the range for medical practice B.'

_____

_____

_____

2 The cumulative frequency graph shows information about the mass of a random sample of 80 eggs from a day's production on farm A.

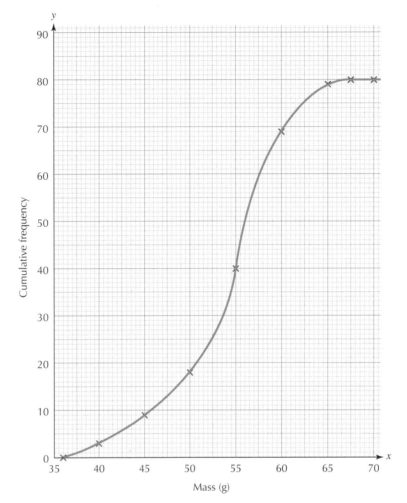

a Use the cumulative frequency graph to estimate the interquartile range.

_____

_____

b Use the cumulative frequency graph to estimate the number of eggs that weigh between 55 and 60 grams.

_____

_____

c The farmer at farm A can only sell eggs that weigh at least 45 grams.

What percentage of the eggs **cannot** be sold?

_____

_____

d Work out the probability that an egg chosen at random weighs 60 grams or more.

_____

_____

e Another farmer, at farm B, has these summary statistics for the mass of the eggs produced by his hens, using a sample of 10 eggs.

Minimum	LQ	Median	UQ	Maximum
32 g	53 g	54 g	60 g	66 g

He says: 'My hens lay bigger eggs than the hens at farm A.'

By comparing the data, explain whether you think his argument is correct.

_____

_____

_____

_____

3 Hector sowed a packet of 200 radish seeds. On the packet, the seed company claims that 75% of the seeds will produce a radish of at least 60 mm in length.

Hector planted all 200 seeds. Only 150 of the seeds grew into a radish.

He produced this cumulative frequency graph to show information about the full grown length of the 150 radishes.

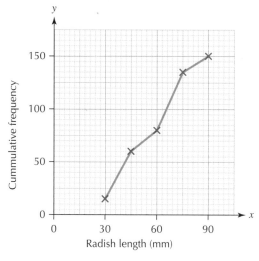

a Make one criticism of Hector's graph.

_____

_____

b Use the cumulative frequency graph, and the information given, to work out the probability that a seed chosen at random from the packet of seeds will produce a radish of at least 60 mm in length.

Compare your answer with the claim on the seed packet.

_____

_____

_____

_____

5.2 Histograms 🖩

Hint: In a histogram, the area of each bar represents the frequency. The height of each bar is the frequency density, where frequency density = $\dfrac{\text{frequency}}{\text{class width}}$.

1 The heights of 100 Year 7 girls are recorded in a table.

Height, h (cm)	$100 < h \leq 110$	$110 < h \leq 125$	$125 < h \leq 135$	$135 < h \leq 150$	$150 < h \leq 155$
Class width					
Frequency	8	33	37	18	4
Frequency density					

a Draw a histogram to display this data.

Hint: Frequency density is always plotted on the vertical axis.

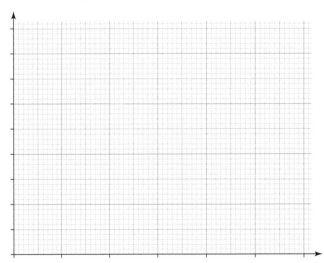

b Use your histogram to estimate the following.

    i The number of Year 7 girls who are less than 1.4 m tall

Hint: Draw a vertical line from 140 cm on the height axis to the top of the rectangle for the interval $135 < h \leqslant 150$, then find the total area of all the rectangles to the left of this line.

_____

_____

_____

_____

_____

    ii The median height

_____

   iii The interquartile range

_____

_____

_____

_____

_____

Hint: For a set of n data items, the position of the median is the $\frac{n+1}{2}$ th value,

the position of the LQ is the $\frac{n+1}{4}$ th value and the position of the UQ is

the $\frac{3(n+1)}{4}$ th value.

- First work out in which interval the median/LQ/UQ lies.
- Then work out the total area of the rectangle needed in this interval to make the total frequency equal to the position of the median.
- Use frequency = frequency density × width to work out the width of the rectangle x.
- Add x to lower bound of interval.

c Estimate the mean height of the Year 7 girls.

Hint: The mean of a grouped frequency distribution $= \frac{\sum fx}{\sum f}$ where x is the midpoint of each interval.

_____

_____

_____

_____

2 The heights of 100 Year 7 boys are recorded in a table.

Height, h (m)	$0.9 < h \leqslant 1.05$	$1.05 < h \leqslant 1.2$	$1.2 < h \leqslant 1.3$	$1.3 < h \leqslant 1.35$	$1.35 < h \leqslant 1.5$
Frequency	21	30	30	10	9

a Draw a histogram to display this data.

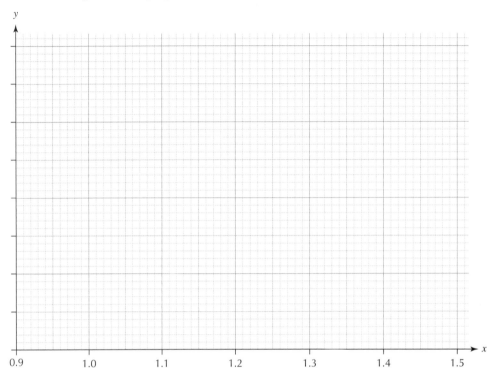

b Use your histogram to estimate the following.

   i The number of Year 7 boys who are taller than 1 m 10 cm

_____

   ii The median height

_____

   iii The interquartile range

_____

_____

c Estimate the mean height of the boys.

_____

_____

3 The incomplete table and histogram below give some information about the masses of 80 cherry tomatoes.

Mass, m (grams)	$3 < m \leq 4$	$4 < m \leq 6$	$6 < m \leq 8$	$8 < m \leq 11$	$11 < m \leq 15$
Frequency	2	6			12

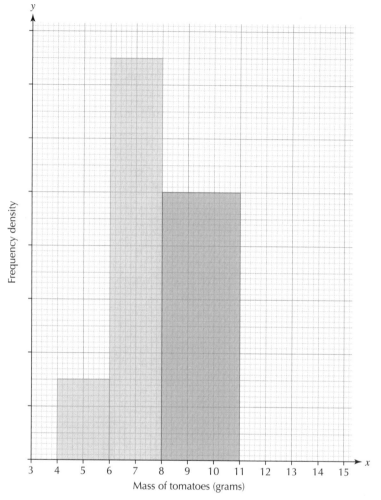

Mass of tomatoes (grams)

a Cherry tomatoes are classified as too large if they weigh more than 12 grams. Estimate the number of tomatoes that are too large.

_____

_____

b Cherry tomatoes are classified as too small if they weigh less than 4.5 grams. Estimate the number of tomatoes that are too small.

_____

_____

4

Company A

Class interval (£000)	Frequency
$0 < x \leqslant 20$	18
$20 < x \leqslant 40$	50
$40 < x \leqslant 80$	51
$80 < x \leqslant 100$	6

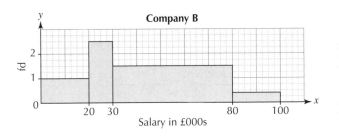

The salaries of a random sample of 125 employees from Company A and 125 employees from Company B were recorded.

The frequency table and the histogram show the information for each company.

a Draw a suitable histogram for Company A.

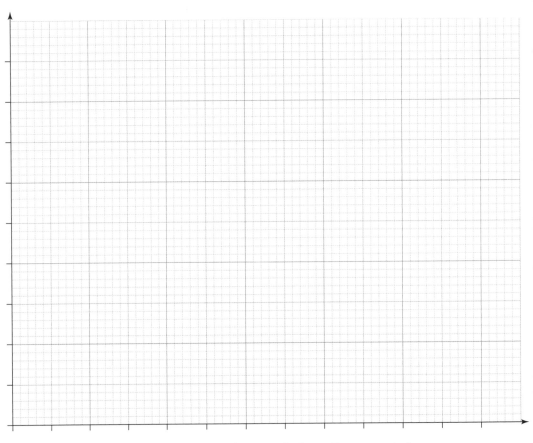

b Estimate the number of employees in the sample from Company A that earn between £30 000 and £80 000.

_____

_____

_____

c Comment on the differences in the distributions of salaries for Company A and Company B.

_____

_____

_____

_____

5.3 Sampling 🖩

Hint: In a **random sample**, every member of the population has an equal chance of being chosen.

1 The table shows the students in a school by gender and year group.

Year group	Girls	Boys	Total
7	124	126	250
8	127	132	259
9	136	151	287
10	144	156	300
11	144	170	314
Total	**675**	**735**	**1410**

The head teacher wants to survey 100 of these students.

a Which of the three methods below would give a random sample?

i Asking four Year 8 maths classes with 25 students in each class.

ii Asking the first 100 students who arrive at school in the morning.

iii Putting students in alphabetical order by name, giving each a number from 1 to 1410, putting tickets numbered 1 to 1410 into a bucket, then picking out 100 tickets.

b Explain your choice and give a reason why the other methods would not be suitable as a random sample.

Hint: Do not just write, for example, 'It will be biased.' You must explain _why_ it will be biased.

_____

_____

_____

_____

_____

2 The head of mathematics suggests that selecting a sample stratified by gender and year group would be a better method.

> Hint: In a stratified sample you select the number to represent each of the strata, using $\dfrac{\text{sample size}}{\text{population size}} \times$ strata size. You need to round your answer to the nearest whole number.

a Explain why stratified sampling would be a more suitable method.

_____

_____

_____

b Work out the number of each strata that should be in the sample of 100 students.

_____

_____

_____

3 There are 288 students from six nations in a European school.

The head teacher wants to select a sample of these students to complete a survey.

He decides to select a sample of 24 students stratified by nation.

Complete the table to show how many students from each country should be in the sample.

Country	Students	Sample size
Belgium	30	
France	50	
Germany	72	
Luxembourg	12	
Netherlands	40	
Italy	84	

4 A researcher wants to investigate the number of otters in a conservation area using the capture–recapture method.

He visits the conservation area and catches 30 otters and marks them with a tag.

One month later he revisits the conservation area and captures 40 otters.

He finds that six of them are tagged.

Estimate how many otters are in the conservation area.

Hint: The capture–recapture method uses proportion to estimate the size of the population, N, of an animal species.

$$\frac{n}{N} = \frac{m}{M}$$

where:

n is the number in the first sample that are tagged

M is the size of the second sample

m is the number in the second sample that are tagged.

_____

_____

_____

5.4 Sample space diagrams and experimental probability

Hint: A sample space diagram shows all the possible outcomes of two events.

1 Four cards and a fair coin are used in a game.

The four cards are the 2 of spades, 4 of spades, 8 of clubs and 10 of hearts.

A card is chosen at random and the coin is tossed.

A player scores the number on the card multiplied by:

- 2 if the coin lands on heads
- 1 if the coin lands on tails.

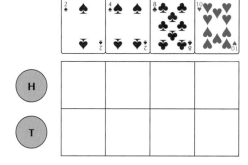

a Complete the scores for the sample space diagram.

b What is the probability of getting a score greater than 8?

_____

_____

c Kerry plays the game 20 times. How many times would you expect her to get a score greater than 8?

> Hint: Expected number of outcomes = number of trials × probability

_____

_____

2 A game is played where you roll two dice and add the number on each dice to get your score.

If your score is 6 or less you earn 10 points. If your score is more than 6 you earn 0 points.

a What is the probability that you score 6 or less?

_____

b What is the probability that you earn 20 points after your first two rolls of the dice?

_____

In a different version of the game, three dice are rolled and the numbers on each dice are added to get your score. In this game, if you score 9 or less you earn 10 points. If your score is more than 9 you earn 0 points.

c How many different outcomes are there in this game?

_____

d In which version of the game is it easier to earn 10 points? Explain your answer.

_____

_____

3 A train starts at Brighton station and travels to London Victoria station.

The train makes one stop on the journey, at Gatwick Airport station.

Brighton — Gatwick Airport — London Victoria

A total of 60 passengers buy rail tickets at Brighton and board the train.

At Gatwick Airport:

- 40% of these passengers leave the train
- 50 more passengers buy rail tickets and board the train.

All the passengers on the train when it arrives at London Victoria leave the train.

a Work out the probability that a passenger picked at random:

i boarded the train at Brighton and left the train at London Victoria

_____

ii boarded the train at Brighton and left the train at Gatwick Airport.

_____

20% of the rail tickets bought by the passengers at Brighton and Gatwick Airport were first class. The rest of the rail tickets were standard class.

b Work out the probability that a passenger travelling with a first class ticket boarded the train:

    i   at Brighton and left the train at Gatwick Airport

    _____

    ii at Gatwick Airport.

    _____

c Work out the probability that a passenger travelling with a standard class ticket boarded the train at Brighton and left the train at London Victoria.

_____

4 A manufacturer of light bulbs claims that 92% of the light bulbs they produce last for longer than 25 000 hours. The light bulbs are sold in packs of two.

A shop buys 500 packs of light bulbs. Work out an estimate for the number of packs of light bulbs that will have exactly one light bulb that lasts longer than 25 000 hours.

_____

_____

_____

5.5 Conditional probability and tree diagrams 🖩

Hint: Two events are dependent if the outcome of one event depends on the outcome of another event.

Conditional probability is the probability of a dependent event.

1 The 12 picture cards in a pack of 52 playing cards are laid face down on a table.

♥ K	♠ K	♦ K	♣ K
♥ Q	♠ Q	♦ Q	♣ Q
♥ J	♠ J	♦ J	♣ J

Two cards are chosen at random **without replacement**.

a What is the probability of picking two kings? _____

b What is the probability of picking two red cards? _____

c What is the probability of picking two black queens? _____

d What is the probability of picking a red jack and a black king? _____

2 Two speakers were chosen at random from a group of four German speakers and seven English speakers.

Using a tree diagram, show that the probability of selecting one German speaker and one English speaker from the group is just over 50%.

3 The word 'RECEIVE' is made by using letters written on seven cards.

Three cards are chosen at random without replacement.

Show that the probability of choosing three vowels is twice that of choosing two consonants and one vowel.

_____

_____

_____

_____

◎ **4** Two jars, A and B, contain coloured balls.

Jar A contains 4 white, 4 red, 3 blue and 1 green.

Jar B contains 3 white, 3 red, 3 blue and 1 green.

a One ball is chosen at random from each jar.

   i What is the probability that both balls are red?

_____

   ii What is the probability that both balls are the same colour?

_____

b Write the following as a ratio in its simplest form:

  probability of two balls being the same : probability of two balls being different.

_____

c Two balls are chosen at random from each jar without replacement.

  What is the probability that all four balls are the same colour?

_____

5 Consider two tables, A and B. On each table, three cards are lying face down. The value of each card is shown in the diagram.

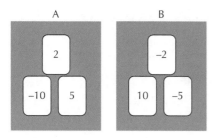

Two cards are drawn from table A without being replaced.

The value of the second card is added to the first card to give result x.

Two cards are then randomly selected from table B.

The value of the first card is subtracted from result x and then this result is multiplied by the value of the second card.

a Calculate the probability that the result is greater than 0.

_____

b Calculate the probability that the result is less than or equal to 20.

_____

6 In a raffle, 360 tickets are sold.

Four of the tickets are picked to win a prize.

Ellie buys a ticket for the raffle.

What is the probability that she will win at least one prize?

> Hint: P(event happens at least once) = 1 − P(event does not happen)

_____

_____

_____

_____

_____

5.6 Venn diagrams and mutually exclusive events

1. At a school, 120 students were sampled in a survey.

   Some of the students sampled study French or German but not both.

   Some of the students study English.

   85 students study French and English, seven study only English, five do not study French, German or English and 11 study only German.

   The number of students that study German and English is equal to the number of students that only study French.

   a Draw a Venn diagram to show this information.

   b If a student is picked at random, what is the probability that:

   i they study French or English? _____

   ii they only study one or fewer of the three subjects? _____

   iii they study English? _____

   iv they study French or German but not English?

   _____

2. One hundred members of a social media group who love chocolate completed a survey on whether they liked three different chocolate bars: Saturn Delight, S; Lanchunky, L; and Grekumptious, G. A total of 18 said they liked all three; 22 said they liked only L and G; 12 said they liked only S and L; 66 members said they liked G, with x of them stating that they only liked G; 42 said they liked S; $\frac{x}{12}$ only liked G and S. The number of people who only liked S was $\frac{5x}{12}$ and five said they didn't like any of them.

a Draw a Venn diagram to show this information.

ξ

b What is the probability that, in a random selection, a person from the group likes:

i only L? _____

ii only S? _____

iii none of the three chocolate bars? _____

iv only two bars of chocolate? _____

> Hint: Parts **c** and **d** are examples of **conditional** probability.

c Given that a person likes G, what is the probability they also like L?

_____

_____

d Given that a person likes L, what is the probability they also like S?

_____

3 60 children attend a sports summer school.

They can choose to do any combination of football, F, gymnastics, G or swimming, S.

20 children chose to do football only.

10 children chose to do gymnastics only.

13 children chose to do swimming only.

6 children chose football and gymnastics.

10 children chose football and swimming.

9 children chose gymnastics and swimming.

a Draw a Venn diagram to show this information.

> **Hint:** Let *x* represent the number that chose all three activities.

b How many children chose all three activities?

_____

> **Hint:** For sets A and B, A ∩ B (read as A intersection B) represents all the elements that are in set A AND set B; A ∪ B (read as A union B) represents all the elements that are in set A OR set B.
>
>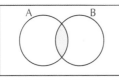
>
> | |
> | The intersection is where two sets overlap. |
> | A ∩ B |
> | This means A and B. |
> | **AND rule** |
>
>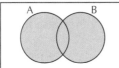
>
> | |
> | If you put two sets together, you get the **Union**. |
> | A ∪ B |
> | This means A or B. |
> | **OR rule** |
>
> A′ means all the elements **not** in A.
>
> ξ means the universal set.

c Work out:

i P(F ∩ G ∩ S _____

ii P(F ∪ G) _____

iii P(S′) _____

d Given that a child chose gymnastics, work out the probability they also chose football.

> **Hint:** The probability that a child also chose football given that they chose gymnastics can be written in set notation as P(F | G)

_____

_____

6 Problem solving

1 The diagram shows two right-angled triangles ABC and CDE.

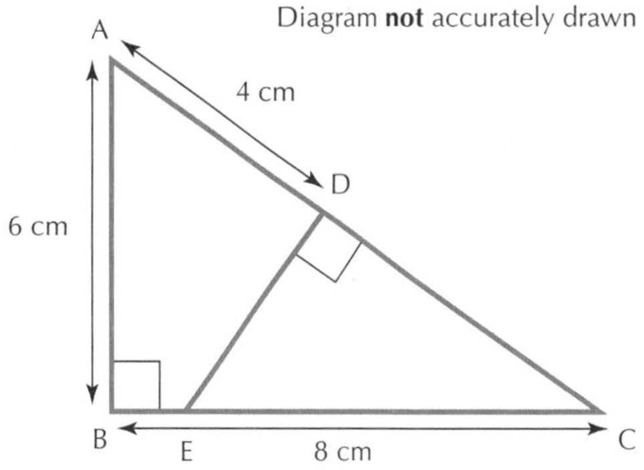

   a Find the length of the line DE and hence the area of quadrilateral ABED.

Diagram **not** accurately drawn

_____

_____

_____

_____

(5 marks)

   b Work out the ratio of the area of triangle ABC to the area of triangle EDC.

_____

_____

(2 marks)

2 **a** A train of length 175 m is travelling at 114 km/h as it approaches a tunnel of length 1.25 km.

     How long will it take the train to pass completely through the tunnel at this speed?

_____

_____

_____

(3 marks)

   b Trains consist of two different types of vehicle: one 15 m locomotive and a number of 20 m passenger carriages.

     Work out how long it would take a train consisting of a locomotive and six passenger carriages to pass through the tunnel, at the following velocities.

     i At 114 km/h

_____

_____

_____

(3 marks)

ii At x km/h

_____

_____

_____

(4 marks)

3 The diagram shows a square, of side length x. Inside the square is a triangle with a vertex at a perpendicular distance y from the top edge of the square.

Given that the ratio of the area of the triangle to the area of the square is 3 : 8, find y in terms of x.

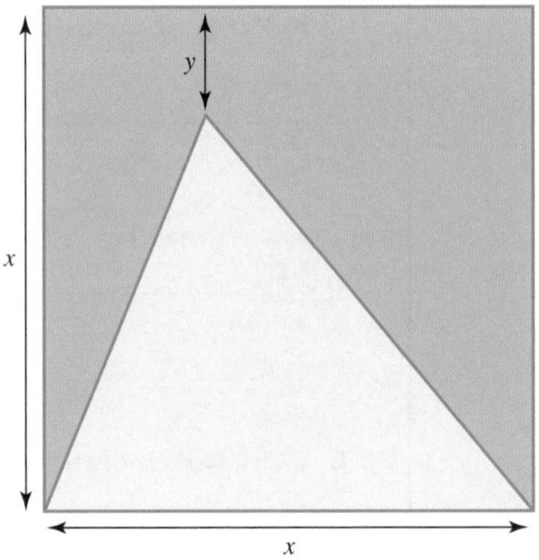

_____

_____

_____

_____

_____

_____

_____

_____

_____

_____

_____

_____

_____

_____

_____

_____

(4 marks)

4 The diagrams show a workbench with two identical wooden cuboids, A and B, placed in different positions.

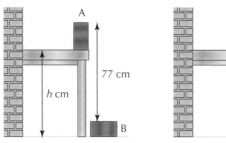

Diagram **not** accurately drawn

Calculate the height, h, of the workbench.

_____

_____

_____

_____

_____

_____

_____

_____

_____

_____

_____

_____

_____

_____

_____

_____

_____

(7 marks)

5 A glass test tube is made up of a cylinder and a hemisphere, as shown.

4 cm

Diagram **not** accurately drawn

16 cm

a Work out the total volume of the test tube. Give your answer in terms of π.

_____

_____

_____

_____

_____

_____

(5 marks)

The test tube is filled with a chemical to a depth d cm, as shown.

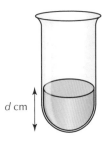

d cm

The chemical occupies exactly one-third of the full capacity of the test tube.

b Work out the value of d, correct to the nearest millimetre.

_____

_____

_____

_____

_____

_____

(6 marks)

6 Alex is working with this equation: $y = \dfrac{10x - 5}{\sqrt{16 - 9x^2}}$.

She wants to draw a graph of the equation.

a Alex thinks the graph of the equation will only intersect the x-axis once.

Explain why she is correct.

_____

_____

_____

(2 marks)

b Explain why Alex cannot find a value for y when x is $\dfrac{4}{3}$.

_____

_____

_____

(2 marks)

c Write down another value of x for which a value of y cannot be found.

Explain your answer.

_____

_____

_____

(2 marks)

7 ABCDEFGH is a regular octagon, of side length 1 cm.

a Calculate the exact length of AD.

_____

_____

_____

_____

Diagram **not** accurately drawn

_____

_____

_____

(7 marks)

b Prove that lines AH and BG are parallel.

_____

_____

_____

_____

_____

_____

_____

(5 marks)

8 'Green garden' paint is made by mixing blue and yellow paint in the ratio 3 : 1.

'Green gold' paint is made by mixing blue and yellow paint in the ratio 1 : 3.

One litre of Green garden paint is mixed with half a litre of Green gold paint by mistake.

How much blue paint needs to be added to this mixture to make it in the correct ratio for Green garden paint?

_____

_____

_____

_____

_____

_____

_____

_____

(6 marks)

9 This is a right-angled trapezium-shaped tile.

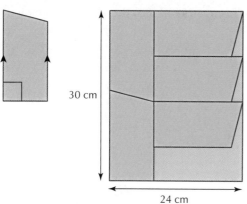

30 cm

24 cm

Diagram **not** accurately drawn

Five of these tiles are arranged inside a blue rectangle that measures 24 cm by 30 cm.
Calculate the area of the blue rectangle that is still visible.

_____

_____

_____

_____

_____

_____

_____

_____

_____

_____

_____

_____

_____

_____

_____

_____

_____

(6 marks)

10 The sketch shows three identical rectangles with their sides parallel to the axes.

Find the coordinates of point X and hence the area of the shape made by the three rectangles.

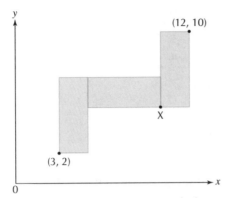

Diagram **not** accurately drawn

_____

_____

_____

_____

_____

(6 marks)

11 Find the coordinates of the point where these two lines would meet if they were extended.

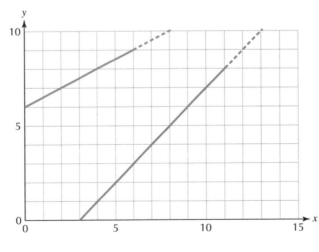

_____

_____

_____

_____

_____

_____

(8 marks)

12 A hot chocolate machine dispenses 155 millilitres of hot chocolate into cups with a capacity of 190 millilitres.

These values are correct to 3 significant figures.

Milk is supplied in small cartons that contain 16 millilitres, correct to the nearest millilitre.

Jenna likes her drinks to be milky and always adds two small cartons of milk to her hot chocolate.

Could Jenna's cup overflow?

You **must** show your working.

_____

_____

_____

_____

(4 marks)

13 A glass paperweight is in the shape of a cone.

The density of the glass is 2 g/cm³.

The slant height of the cone is 10 cm.

The vertical height of the cone is 6 cm.

Work out the mass of the paperweight, giving your answer in terms of π.

_____

_____

_____

_____

_____

_____

_____

(5 marks)

14 The diagram shows two blue diagonals drawn on the faces of a cube.

Calculate the angle between the blue diagonals.

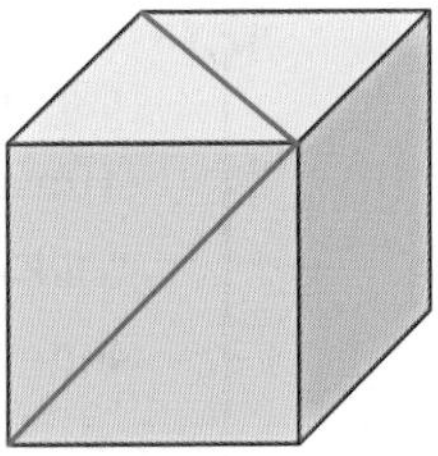

_____

_____

_____

_____

_____

_____

_____

(3 marks)

15 **a** A rectangle is placed symmetrically inside a square.

The rectangle has sides of length a and b.

Show that the area of the square is $\frac{1}{2}(a + b)^2$

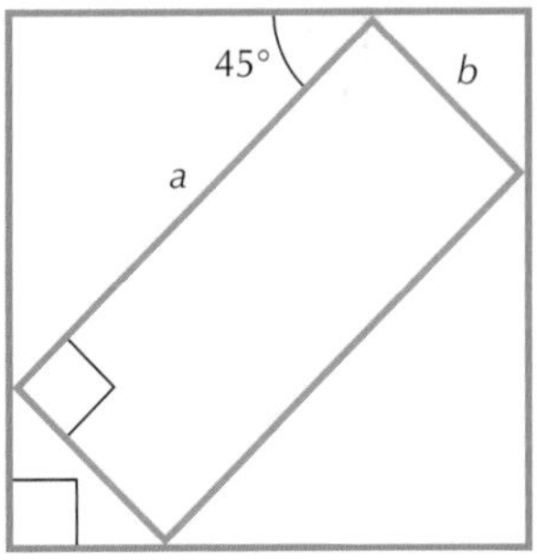

_____

_____

_____

_____

_____

_____

_____

_____

_____

_____

_____

_____

_____

(10 marks)

b A triangle FBD is placed inside a square ACEF.

Length DF is $3\sqrt{17}$ cm and $\tan\theta = 0.25$.

Calculate the total area of the square.

Diagram **not** accurately drawn

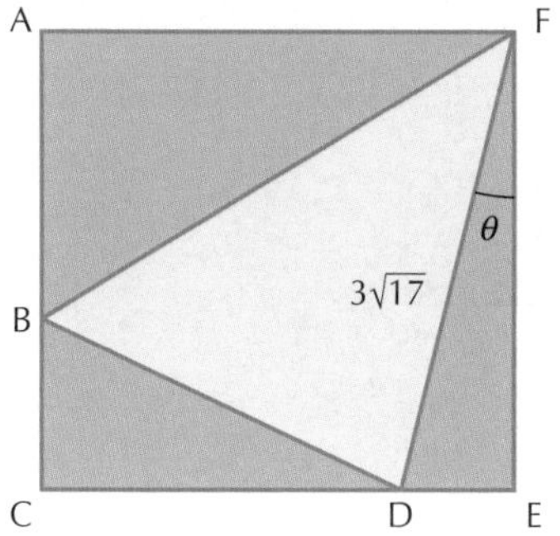

_____

_____

_____

_____

_____

_____

_____

_____

_____

_____

_____

_____

_____

_____

_____

_____

_____

(10 marks)

16 In the diagram, BD : DC = 3 : 2.

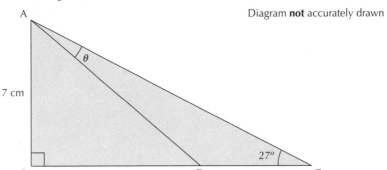

Diagram **not** accurately drawn

a Show that $BC = \dfrac{35}{5\tan 27}$.

_____

_____

_____

_____

_____

_____

(5 marks)

b Calculate angle θ.

_____

_____

(2 marks)

17 ABCDE is a pentagon.

Show that the area of the pentagon is $10\sqrt{15} + 55\sqrt{3}$ cm².

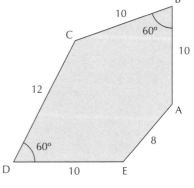

_____

_____

_____

_____

Diagram **not** accurately drawn

_____

_____

(7 marks)

18 Mali is using the quadratic formula to solve a quadratic equation.

After correctly substituting the values, he writes:

$$x = \frac{8 \pm \sqrt{64 - 96}}{6}.$$

a Write down the quadratic equation that Mali is trying to solve.

_____

_____

(3 marks)

b Explain why Mali will not be able to find any solutions to the equation.

_____

_____

(1 mark)

19 Abbie has drawn a sketch of one of her kitchen walls and of one of the tiles she will use to tile it.

The wall has been measured to the nearest 10 cm and the tiles are measured to the nearest 0.5 cm.

Abbie will throw away any partly used tiles, without trying to patch them.

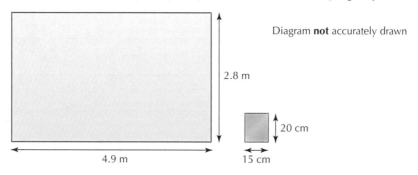

Diagram **not** accurately drawn

2.8 m

20 cm

4.9 m

15 cm

a Work out the minimum number of tiles Abbie needs.

_____

_____

_____

(5 marks)

b How many more tiles than the minimum might she need?

_____

_____

_____

(5 marks)

20 A slice of a circular 10-inch deep-pan pepperoni pizza costs £3.99.

A slice of a circular 14-inch deep-pan pepperoni pizza costs £5.49.

Which of the pizza slices is the better value for money?

You **must** show your working.

10 inch pepperoni

£3.99

120°

14 inch pepperoni

£5.49

90°

_____

_____

_____

_____

_____

_____

_____

_____

_____

_____

_____

(7 marks)

21 **a** The ratio of height : length : depth of this cuboid is 2 : 3 : 4.

The total surface area of the cuboid is 1300 cm².

Find the volume of the cuboid.

_____

_____

_____

_____

height

length

depth

Diagram **not** accurately drawn

_____

_____

_____

(7 marks)

b The ratio of height : length : depth of a different cuboid is $4 : 1 : 2$.

The volume of the cuboid 64 000 cm³.

Find the surface area of this cuboid.

_____

_____

_____

_____

_____

_____

(7 marks)

22 A cube has a side length of 10 cm.

Diagram **not** accurately drawn

Three slices, each of thickness x cm, are cut off the cube, one after another.

A slice of thickness x cm is removed from the right-hand side.

A slice of thickness x cm is then removed from the top.

A slice of thickness x cm is then removed from the front.

What is the volume of the remaining piece, in terms of x?

_____

_____

_____

_____

_____

_____

_____

(6 marks)

23 In triangle ACE, B is the midpoint of AC and D is the midpoint CE.

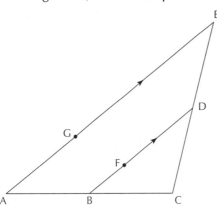

a Prove that the vector $\overrightarrow{BD}$ is parallel to vector $\overrightarrow{AE}$ and find the ratio BD : AE.

_____

_____

_____

_____

(4 marks)

b F is a point on BD such that $\overrightarrow{BF} = \frac{1}{3}\overrightarrow{FD}$ and G is a point on AE such that $\overrightarrow{AG} = \frac{1}{3}\overrightarrow{GE}$.

Prove that the points C, F and G lie on a straight line.

_____

_____

_____

_____

_____

(5 marks)

24 Five cones A, B, C, D and E are mathematically similar.

Their heights are in the ratio 2 : 3 : 4 : 5 : 6.

Cone B has height 3.6 cm and surface area 45 cm².

A   B   C   D   E

Diagram **not** accurately drawn

a Work out the height of cone C.

_____

_____

_____

_____

(2 marks)

b Work out the surface area of cone D.

_____

_____

_____

_____

(3 marks)

c Cone A is used to fill cone E with sand.

How many full cones of sand from cone A are needed to completely fill cone E?

_____

_____

_____

_____

(3 marks)

7 Spot the errors

In each of the questions in this section, look at the two students' responses and identify any errors in the working.

Some responses have more than one error. Identify the errors in the book then work out the correct answer for each question.

1 When diesel fuel is sold, the money from the sale is divided in the following ratio.

Tax	:	Oil company	:	Petrol station
77	:	43	:	5

a How many pence in every pound goes to the petrol station? (3 marks)

b One week, a petrol station sells £40 300 worth of diesel fuel.

   i How much of the £40 300 goes to the oil company? (2 marks)

   ii The amount £40 300 was rounded to the nearest £10.

The cost of diesel fuel is 122p per litre, to the nearest penny.

Calculate the maximum number of litres of diesel fuel sold that week. (3 marks)

> **Hint:** The first answer has been marked, to show you what to do.

A1

Arnold

a $77 + 43 + 5 = 125$ p ✓

$125 - 25 = 100p = £1$ ✗ $\dfrac{5}{125} \times 100$ (5p out of 125p → petrol station)

so 25p   so 4p

 Need all 3 parts of the ratio.

b i $\dfrac{43}{77+5} \times 40\,300 = £21\,132.93$ ✗ $\dfrac{43}{125} \times 40\,300 = £13\,863.20$

   ii $40\,310 \div 1.21 = 33\,314$ litres ✗ $\dfrac{40\,305}{1.215} = 33\,173$ litres

(nearest litre)

Incorrect bounds used.

A1

Ziggi

a $77 + 43 + 5 = 125$

so $5 \times \dfrac{125}{100} = 6.25\,p$

b i $\dfrac{77 + 5}{125} \times 40\,300 = £26\,436.80$

   ii $40\,305 \div 121.5 = 331.72$ litres

---

2 Prove that the difference between the squares of two consecutive even numbers is twice the sum of the numbers.

(5 marks)

A2

Ian

$4^2 - 2^2 = 12$ and $2 \times (4 + 2) = 12$

$6^2 - 4^2 = 20$ and $2 \times (6 + 4) = 20$

$8^2 - 6^2 = 28$ and $2 \times (8 + 6) = 28$

They always go up in 8s so they will always work.

A2

Priya

The first even number is $2n$ so the one below it is $2n - 2$

$2n^2 - 2n^2 - 2 = 2 \times (2n + 2n - 2)$

$-2n = 8n - 4$

$2 = 8n$

$8 \div 2 = 4$, which is even.

---

3 A company sells single gold earrings in different sizes.

The earrings are circular.

The price of each earring is proportional to the square of its radius.

The price of an earring of radius 1.5 cm is £7.50. What is the price of an earring of radius 3 cm?

(5 marks)

A3

Kristel

The radius of the square earring is double, so

$£7.50 \times 2 = £15$

A3

Tariq

$p \propto r^2$

$p = kr^2$

$1.5 = k \times 7.5^2$

$k = 0.26666$

$p = 0.26666r^2$

$p = 0.26666 \times 3^2$

$p = £24$

4 a and b are integers such that $a > 0$, $b > 0$ and

$$\sqrt{a^2 + 8b} = 11$$
$$\sqrt{a^2 - 16b} = 1.$$

Calculate the value of $\sqrt{a^2 - ab}$. (6 marks)

A4

Sanjay

$a + 4b = 11$ ①

$a - 8b = 1$ ②

① − ② gives

$-4b = 10$

$\underline{b = -2.5}$

so $a + -4 \times 2.5 = 11$

$a - 10 = 11$

$\underline{a = 21}$

so

$$\sqrt{a^2 - ab} = \sqrt{21^2 - 21 \times -2.5} = 13.1339255\ldots$$

A4

Charlie

$a^2 + 8b = 121$

$a^2 - 16b = 1$

$24b = 120$

$b = 5$

$a^2 + 8 \times 5 = 121$

$a^2 + 40 = 121$

$a^2 = 81$

$a = 9$

so $\sqrt{a^2} - ab = \sqrt{9^2} - 9 \times 5 = -36$

5 This right-angled triangle has sides of length y cm, x cm and $(x + 1)$ cm.

x and y are both integers.

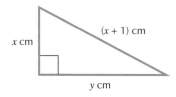

Prove that y must be an odd number. (4 marks)

A5

Gianni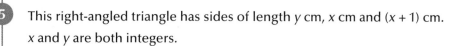

Pythagorean triples

$y = 3$, $x = 4$, $x + 1 = 4 + 1 = 5$ and $3^2 + 4^2 = 5^2$

$y = 5$, $x = 12$, $x + 1 = 12 + 1 = 13$ and $5^2 + 12^2 = 13^2$

$y = 7$, $x = 24$, $x + 1 = 24 + 1 = 25$ and $7^2 + 12^2 = 13^2$

y is always an odd number because there must be loads more of these.

A5

Cheryl

$x^2 + y^2 = (x + 1)^2$

$x^2 + y^2 = x^2 + 2x + 1$

$y^2 = 2x + 1$

which is the same as $2n + 1$, which is odd, so y must be odd.

6 Prove that $\dfrac{\sqrt{20} + 10}{\sqrt{5}} = 2\left(1 + \sqrt{5}\right)$. (4 marks)

A6

Leo

Left-hand side

$$= \frac{\sqrt{20}}{\sqrt{5}} + 10$$

$$= \sqrt{4} + 10$$

$$= 2 + 10$$

$$= 12$$

Both sides = 12, proved

Right-hand side

$$= 2 + \sqrt{5}^{2}$$

$$= 2 + 10$$

$$= 12$$

A6

Roxy

$$\frac{\sqrt{20} + 10}{\sqrt{5}} = 2\left(1 + \sqrt{5}\right) \div \text{by } 2$$

$$\frac{\sqrt{10} + 5}{\sqrt{5}} = \left(1 + \sqrt{5}\right) \times \text{by } \sqrt{5}$$

$$\sqrt{10} + 5 = \sqrt{5} + 2\sqrt{5}$$

$$\sqrt{10} + 5 = 3\sqrt{5}$$

$$2\sqrt{5} + 5 = 3\sqrt{5}$$

$$3\sqrt{5} = 3\sqrt{5}$$

LHS = RHS, proved

7 A bag contains two red counters and eight blue counters.

A counter is drawn from the bag at random and not replaced; then a second counter is drawn.

Find the probability that the second counter drawn is red. (5 marks)

A7

Sophie

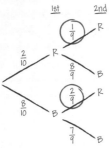

Probability that 2nd is red $= \dfrac{1}{9} + \dfrac{2}{9} = \dfrac{3}{9}$

A7
Asim

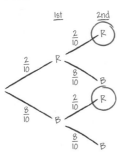

Probability that 2nd is red $\dfrac{2}{10} \times \dfrac{2}{10} + \dfrac{8}{10} \times \dfrac{8}{10} = \dfrac{4}{100} + \dfrac{64}{100} = \dfrac{68}{100}$

8 An even number can be written as $2n$, where n is an integer.

Show that the square of the sum of three consecutive even numbers is $36(n + 1)^2$.

Is it possible for this sum to be 6 084?

If so, find the even integers. If not, explain why it is not possible. (5 marks)

A8

Sanji

$2n$, $2n + 2$ and $2n + 4$

$(2n + 2n + 2 + 2n + 4)^2 = (6n + 6)^2$

$(6n + 6)^2 = 6(n + 1)^2$

$6084 = 6(n + 1)^2$

$1024 = (n + 1)^2$

$32 = n + 1$

$31 = n$

62, 64 and 66

A8

Koli

$2n$, $2n + 2$ and $2n + 4$ are three consecutive numbers

$(2n + 2n + 2 + 2n + 4)^2 = (6n + 6)^2$

$(6n + 6)^2 = 36n^2 + 72n + 36$

$\qquad = 36(n^2 + 2n + 1)$

$\qquad = 36(n + 1)^2$

$6084 = 36(n + 1)^2$

$\therefore 169 = (n + 1)^2$

$13 = n + 1$

$n = 12$

The numbers are 12, 14 and 16.

9 Solve the simultaneous equations

$x^2 + 2x + 4 = y \quad ①$

$2x - 1 + y = 0 \quad ②$

(4 marks)

A9

Tim

Add together

$x^2 + 4x + 4 + 1 - y = y$

$x^2 + 4x + 5 = 0 \quad ③$

$③ - ① \quad 2x + 1 = y$

Substitute y into ②

$4x = 0$

$\therefore x = 0$

Substitute into ①

$y = 4$

Solution when $x = 0$, $y = 4$

A9

Lee

Let $③ = ① - ②$

$\therefore x^2 + 5 = 2y$ ③

Make y the subject of eqn ②

$y = 1 - 2x$

Substitute into eqn ③

$x^2 + 5 = 2(1 - 2x)$

$x^2 + 5 = 2 - 4x$

$x^2 + 4x + 3 = 0$

Complete the square

$x^2 + 4x = -3$

$(x + 2)^2 = -3$

$x + 2 = \sqrt{-3}$

There is no solution to this simultaneous equation as we cannot take the root of -3.

 10 A regular tetrahedron, with edges of length x cm has the same surface area, correct to 4 significant figures, as a sphere with diameter 8 cm.

Calculate the length of x, giving your answer correct to 3 significant figures. (4 marks)

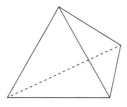 

A10

Hansi

The surface area of a sphere with diameter 8 cm is

$4\pi r^2 = 201.4$ (4 sf)

The surface area of the tetrahedron is 4 times the area of a equilateral triangle with sides x.

The faces are equilateral triangles; length of each side is x.

All angles are 60° therefore

$$\text{area} = \frac{1}{2}ab\sin C$$

$$\therefore = \frac{1}{2}x^2\frac{\sqrt{3}}{2} = x^2\frac{\sqrt{3}}{4}$$

Surface area of the tetrahedron, therefore is

Surface area (tetrahedron) =	Surface area (sphere)
$x^2\sqrt{3}$	201.1

Therefore if

$$x^2\sqrt{3} = 201.1$$

then

$$x^2 = \frac{201.1\sqrt{3}\pi}{3} = 116.1$$

$$x = \sqrt{\left(\frac{16\sqrt{3}\pi}{3}\right)}$$

$$x = 10.8 \text{ cm (3 sf)}$$

A10

Caleb

Area of one triangle in the tetrahedron is

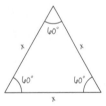 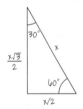

$$\text{Area of triangle} = \frac{\frac{x\sqrt{3}}{2} \times x}{2} = \frac{x^2\sqrt{3}}{4}$$

Therefore area of tetrahedron $= 4\dfrac{x^2\sqrt{3}}{4} = x^2\sqrt{3}$

Area of a sphere $= 4\pi r^2$

Area of this sphere $= 64\pi$

Therefore $64\pi = x^2\sqrt{3}$

Squaring both sides $4096\pi = 3x^2$

$$\therefore \sqrt{\frac{4096\pi}{3}} = x$$

x is 65.5 cm³ (3 sf)

11 The histogram shows some information about the results of an arithmetic test for a group of 20 students. The marks are out of 20.

Draw a frequency density table for this data and work out the frequencies for each interval.

Work out an estimate for the median score. (7 marks)

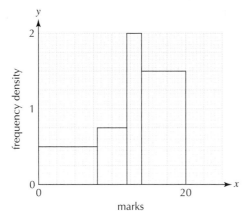

A11

Jacob

Class interval, pupils	Frequency	Frequency density
$0 \leqslant P < 8$	4	0.5
$8 \leqslant P < 12$	3	0.75
$12 < P \leqslant 14$	4	2
$14 \leqslant P < 20$	9	1.5

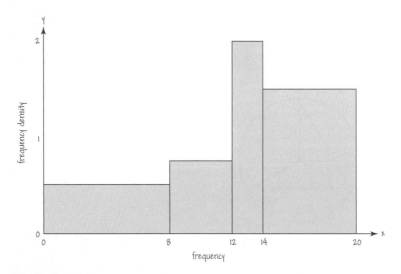

8 pupils score 4 marks, 4 pupils score 3 marks, 2 pupils score 4 marks and 6 pupils score 9 marks. This data placed in order reads 3, 4, 4, 9 and therefore the median mark is 4.

A11

Marjie

Class interval, marks	Frequency	Frequency density
$0 \leqslant m < 8$	4	0.5
$8 \leqslant m < 12$	3	0.75
$12 \leqslant m < 13$	4	2
$14 \leqslant m < 20$	9	1.5

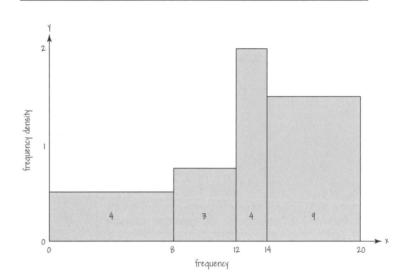

The 10th position is good enough for the median out of 20 and this lies in the class interval 12–14 and so the median is $\dfrac{(12 + 14)}{2} = 13$ marks.

12 O is the centre of the circle.

Angle DCA = 128°

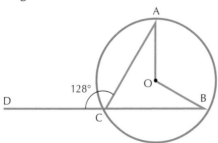

Work out the size of the reflex angle AOB.

You **must** show your working.

(5 marks)

A12

Zac

A = 128° (alternate angle theorem)

A = B = 128° (symmetrical)

C = 180° − 128° = 52° (angles on a straight line)

Angle at O = 360° − 128° − 128° − 52°

$\qquad$ = 52° (quadrilateral = 360°)

Reflex angle = 360° − 52°

$\qquad$ = 308° (reflex angle bigger than 180°)

A12

Cara

C = 60° (triangle ABC is equilateral)

Reflex angle = 180 − 60

$\qquad$ = 120 (opposite angles in cyclic quadrilateral = 180°)

13 A triangle BDF sits inside a square ABCDEF.

The length BF is $\sqrt{89}$ cm, the length DF is $2\sqrt{17}$ cm, the lengths AB and DE are integer values and tan $\theta = 0.25$.

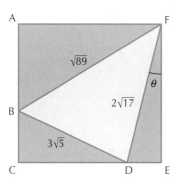

a Calculate the area of triangle DEF. (3 marks)

b Calculate the area of square ABCDEF. (2 marks)

c Calculate the area of triangle BDF. (3 marks)

A13

Simon

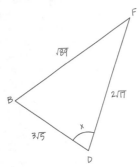

a If $\tan \theta = 0.25 = \frac{1}{4}$ then $DE = 1$ and $EF = 4$.

DE is an integer, in this case it is 1.

Area of the triangle DEF is

$$2\sqrt{17} = \sqrt{x^2 + (4x)^2} = \sqrt{17x^2}$$

$$2\sqrt{17} = x\sqrt{17}$$

$$\therefore x = 2$$

Area is 8 cm²

b If $x = 2$ then area is 64 cm².

c

$$\cos x = \frac{\left(2\sqrt{17}\right)^2 + \left(3\sqrt{5}\right)^2 - \left(\sqrt{89}\right)^2}{2 \times \left(3\sqrt{17}\right) \times \left(3\sqrt{5}\right)}$$

$$\cos^{-1} x = 77.5°$$

A13

Nelson

If $\tan \theta = \frac{1}{4}$ then $DE = x$ and $FE = 4x$.

When you square these sides they are equal

to $\left(2\sqrt{17}\right)^2$ so $x^2 + 16x^2 = 17x^2$ and therefore

if $\left(\sqrt{17}\right)^2 = 17x^2$ then $2\sqrt{17} = 17x^2$ so $x = 2$.

a Area of triangle DEF is $\dfrac{8 \times 1}{2} = 4$ cm²

b Area of square ABCDEF = 64 cm² as each side = 8 cm

c

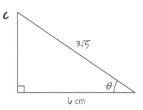

If $CE = 8$ and $DE = 2$ then $CD = 6$ cm

$\sin \theta = \dfrac{6}{3\sqrt{5}}, \therefore \theta = 63.4°$

Area of triangle is $\dfrac{1}{2} ab \sin C$

$= \dfrac{1}{2} \times 6 \times 3\sqrt{5} \sin 63.4 = 18.01°$

8 Answers

ANSWERS TO CHAPTER 1: NUMBER

1.1 Estimating powers and roots

1 **a** 81 **b** 8 **c** 0.125
   d 3 **e** 3 **f** 0.25

2 **a** 5.8 or 5.9 **b** 14.8 **c** 1.1 or 1.2

3 **a** 31 **b** 151 **c** 219

4 **a** 60 **b** 8 **c** 0.2
   d 14 **e** $\frac{1}{18}$

1.2 Combinations and factors

1 $15 \times 14 \times 13 = 2730$

2 **a** $12 \times 15 = 180$ **b** $27 \times 26 \times 25 = 17550$

3 **a** 15 **b** 90
   c $M + C = 6 \times 3 = 18$, $M + V = 6 \times 5 = 30$,
   $V + C = 5 \times 3 = 15$; $18 + 30 + 15 = 63$

4 **a**

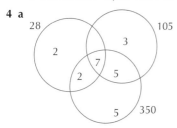

   b i HCF = 7 LCM = 420
   ii HCF = 14 LCM = 700
   iii HCF = 35 LCM = 1050
   iv HCF = 7 LCM = 2100

5 **a** Venn diagram must be complete

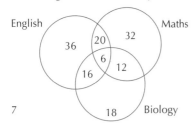

   b 6

1.3 Reverse percentages

1 20 kg 2 $12 million 3 $6 857 143

4 £67 855 5 6.14% increase (3 sf)

6 **a** 2.9% increase **b** £258 212 to nearest £

1.4 Standard form

1 2 kg

2 **a** 135 kg **b i** 60 kg **ii** 1.2×10^4

3 **a** 500 seconds **b** 1.53×10^9 km

4 8.37×10^1

5 1.4×10^{-4} (2 sf)

6 2.95×10^{-4} g

1.5 Bounds

1 **a** Max 3.705; min 3.595 $3.705 \leqslant x + y < 3.595$
   b Max 0.905; min 0.795 $0.795 \leqslant x - y < 0.905$
   c Max 3.26975; min 3.03075 $3.03075 \leqslant xy < 3.26975$
   d Max 1.6703; min 1.5483 $1.5483 \leqslant \frac{x}{y} < 1.6703$

2 No, the maximum size of the card is 12.55 cm
   by 8.5 cm and the minimum size of the envelope
   is 12.5 cm by 9.5 cm, so the card might be
   too long.

3 **a** $45 \div 6.5 = 6.923$ seconds
   b $45 \div 1.325 = 33.96 = 34$ steps

4 $1595 \div 12.05 = 132$

5 Max vol = 3414.53125 cm³; min vol = 3245.20875 cm³
   Max density = 1.231044 g/cm³; min density = 1.16707 g/cm³
   Answers agree to 2 sf so 1.2 g/cm³

1.6 Indices

1 **a** $4^2 = 16$ **b** 4^6 **c** $8^0 = 1$ **d** $2^{-4} = \frac{1}{16}$

2 **a** 1 **b** $\frac{1}{16}$ **c** 5 **d** 0.5
   e 27 **f** $\frac{8}{27}$

3 $n = 2.5$

4 $x = 5$, $y = 2$

5 **a i** xy **ii** x^2 **iii** $\frac{y}{3}$
   b $p = -1$, $q = 4$

1.7 Recurring decimals to fractions

1 **a** $\frac{1}{9}$ **b** $\frac{4}{9}$

2 If $x = 0.\dot{9}$, then $10x = 9.\dot{9}$, $9x = 9$ so $x = 1$. So $0.\dot{9} = 1$.

3 **a** $\frac{23}{99}$ **b** $\frac{1}{45}$ **c** $\frac{73}{300}$ **d** $\frac{367}{1665}$

4 **a** $0.\dot{7}$ **b** $0.9\dot{1}$ **c** $0.3\dot{1}\dot{2}$

1.8 Surds

1 a $\sqrt{15}$ **b** $2\sqrt{15}$

2 a 5 **b** 6 **c** 20
d 12 **e** 10 **f** 3

3 a $2\sqrt{3}$ **b** $4\sqrt{5}$

4 a $6\sqrt{15}$ **b** $18\sqrt{6}$ **c** $4\sqrt{5}$
d 10 **e** $13\sqrt{2}$ **f** $3\sqrt{3}$

5 a 12 **b** 20

6 a $4\sqrt{3}$ **b** $3\sqrt{2}$ **c** $\frac{1}{2}$
d $2(\sqrt{3} - 1)$ or $2\sqrt{3} - 2$

7 a $11 + 6\sqrt{3}$ **b** $\sqrt{3} - 16$ **c** $29 - 4\sqrt{7}$

8 $(\sqrt{15} - \sqrt{12})(\sqrt{15} + \sqrt{12})$
$= 15 + \sqrt{15}\sqrt{12} - \sqrt{12}\sqrt{15} - 12 = 3$

9 $\dfrac{16 + \sqrt{3}}{12}$

10 a $7^2 + (\sqrt{2} + \sqrt{32})^2 = 49 + 2 + 2\sqrt{64} + 32 = 83 + 16 = 99$
and $(3\sqrt{11})^2 = 99$, which satisfies Pythagoras' theorem, so the triangle is right angled.

b $\frac{1}{2} \times 7(\sqrt{2} + \sqrt{32}) = \frac{1}{2} \times 7(\sqrt{2} + 4\sqrt{2}) = \frac{1}{2} \times 7 \times 5\sqrt{2}$
$= \dfrac{35\sqrt{2}}{2}$

11 a $6\sqrt{2}$ **b** $27\sqrt{2}$ **c** 5
d $2\sqrt{30}$ **e** $\dfrac{\sqrt{5}(a - b\sqrt{7})}{5ab}$

ANSWERS TO CHAPTER 2: ALGEBRA

2.1 Solving quadratic equations graphically

1 a $x = -3, x = 1$
b $x = -1$
c $x = -3.2$ to -3.4, $x = 1.2$ to 1.4
d 2

2 a $(1, 6)$
b $x = 3.5, x = -1.45$
c $5 + 2x = x^2$ so $x = \sqrt{2x + 5}$
d 3.449

2.2 Recognising shapes of graphs

1 $y = 2x^2 + 4$ is graph G **2** $y = x^2 + 2x$ is graph D
3 $y = 2x + 4$ is graph A **4** $y = x^3 + 4$ is graph F

5 $y = -x^3 + 4$ is graph E **6** $y = x^2 + 2x + 4$ is graph B
7 $y = \dfrac{4}{x}$ is graph C **8** $y = \cos x$ is graph I
9 $y = \sin x$ is graph H **10** $y = 3^x$ is graph L

2.3 Real-life graphs

1 a 50 km/h² **b** 60 km/h² **c** 35 km/h²
d 75 km **e** 120 km

2 a Each year 9% is added so new amount is 109%, multiplier is 1.09. Repeated for n years so $A \times 1.09^n$.

b
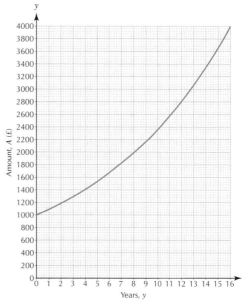

c 13 (12.7 to 12.8) money is added at end of year, so 13 years.

3 a Acceleration increases over the first 10 seconds.
b $a = 3.2$ m/s² (3 to 3.4)
c Approximately 136 m
d Answer is an overestimate as lines for shapes go above curve.
e The more strips you use the more accurate your answer will be.

2.4 Straight lines and their equations

1 a −0.8 **b** (−0.5, −1)
2 a $2y = x - 8$ **b** $2x + 3y + 1 = 0$
3 a $4\sqrt{5}$ **b** $y + 2x = 5$ **c** $2y = x - 10$
4 Lengths of sides are $\sqrt{13}$, $\sqrt{52}$ and $\sqrt{65}$. Using Pythagoras, $12 + 52 = 65$ so right angled.

2.5 Equations of circles and their graphs

1 a $\sqrt{20}$ **b** $x^2 + y^2 = 20$
2 a $\sqrt{5}$ **b** $+\sqrt{12}$ and $-\sqrt{12}$
(y values to 2 dp)

3

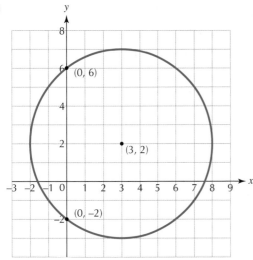

4 a $5^2 + (-3)^2 = 25 + 9 = 34$ **b** $3y = 5x - 34$

5 $\sqrt{14}y = 12 - 2x$

2.6 Functions

1 a 35 **b** 64

2 a $k = 3$ **b** $k = \pm\dfrac{1}{2}$

3 a $3 - 2x^2$ **b** $(3 - 2x)^2$ **c** $3 - \dfrac{8}{x^2}$ **d** $4x - 3$

  e -29 **f** 49 **g** $\dfrac{23}{8}$ **h** -7

4 a $f^{-1}(x) = \dfrac{x - 5}{2}$ **b** $g^{-1}(x) = 4x + 1$

  c $h^{-1}(x) = x^2 + 3$

5 a When $x = -3$ the denominator equals 0 so function does not exist. The graph of $f(x) = \dfrac{x}{x + 3}$ has an asymptote with equation $x = -3$

  b $f^{-1}(x) = \dfrac{3x}{1 - x}$, $f(x) = f^{-1}(x)$ when $x = 0$ and $x = -2$

2.7 Inequalities

1 a 12.5 units² **b** $y \leq 2x - 1$, $y \geq 0$, $2x + y \leq 11$

2 $y < 0.5x + 2$, $y < -2x$ and $y \geq -2$

3

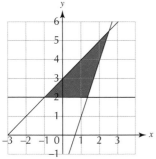

4 a

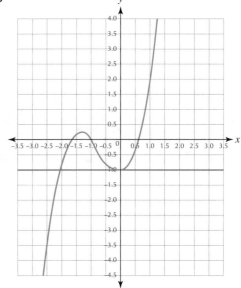

b (2, 5), (3, 3), (3, 4), (4, 3), (5, 2)

c Solutions are all integer pairs of coordinates lying in the region bounded by the curve $xy = 8$ and the line $x + y = 8$.

d $\left(4 - 2\sqrt{2}, 4 + 2\sqrt{2}\right)$ and $\left(4 + 2\sqrt{2}, 4 - 2\sqrt{2}\right)$

2.8 Drawing complex graphs

1 a

x	−2.5	−2	−1	0	1	1.2
x^3	−15.625	−8	−1	0	1	1.728
$+2x^2$	12.5	8	2	0	2	2.88
-1	−1	−1	−1	−1	−1	−1
$y = x^3 + 2x^2 - 1$	−4.125	−1	0	−1	2	3.608

b

c $x = -1.6, -1.0, 0.6$

d Rearrange to give give $x^3 + 2x^2 - 1 = -1$, draw the line $y = -1$ on the graph.

The line intersects at $x = -2$ and is a tangent to the curve when $x = 0$, so there two roots for the equation.

2 a

x	−6	−5	−4	−3	−2	−1	1	2	3	4	5	6
f(x)	0	−0.4	−1	−2	−4	−10	14	8	6	5	4.4	4

b

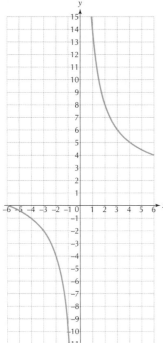

c $x = 0$, $y = 2$

d 5.75

3 a The number of bacteria present at the start.

b

T	0	1	2	3	4	5	6	8	10	12
N	200	400	800	1600	3200	6400	12800	51200	204800	819200

c

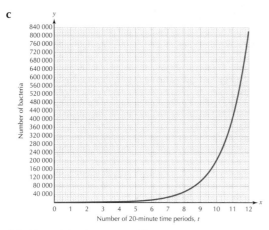

d i About 20000   **ii** 140000 to 150000

e i 180 minutes or 3 hours   **ii** 210 minutes or 3.5 hours

f The number of bacteria would increase more quickly so the answers to part **d** would increase and the answers to part **e** would decrease.

2.9 Areas beneath graphs

1 a (2, −1)   **b** 3   **c** 12 square units

2 a (2, 4)   **b** 8 square units

3 a i Car accelerates from 0 to 15 m/s in 10 s.

    ii Car travels with a constant velocity 15 m/s.

   iii Car decelerates from 15 m/s to 0 in 10 s.

b 450 m

4 a 4 square units

b An underestimate, using two triangles and a rectangle, the edges of shapes lie above the curve.

c Using more strips would give a more accurate estimate for the area.

2.10 Trigonometric graphs

1 a 36°, 144°   **b** 126°, 234°   **c** 88°, 272°

2 a 209°, 331°   **b** 61°, 299°

3 a $x = 45°$ or $x = 135$; $\sin 45° = \cos 45° = \dfrac{\sqrt{2}}{2}$ and

$\sin 225° = \cos 225° = -\dfrac{\sqrt{2}}{2}$

b $x = -135°$, (45°, 225°), 405°, 585°

4 44.2°, 135.6°, 404.2°, 495.6°

5 115.7°, 244.3°, 475.7°, 604.3°

6 a 180°   **b** 60°, 240°, 420°, 600°

2.11 Transformation of functions

1 a B   **b** A   **c** C

Blue line $y = \cos 3x$, orange line $y = \cos(2x + 3)$, purple line $y = 3\cos 2x$

3 a $2f(x)$:   A (−10, 0), B (1, 0), C (5, −6)

b $-3f(x)$:   A (−10, 0), B(1, 0), C (5, 9)

c $\dfrac{1}{2}f(x)$:   A (−10, 0), B (1, 0), C $\left(5, -\dfrac{3}{2}\right)$

d $2f(x - 2)$:   A (−8, 0), B (3, 0), C (7, −6)

e $2f(x) + 1$:   A (−10, 1), B (1, 1), C (5, −5)

4 a $f(x) - 5$:   A (−10, −5), B (1, −5), C (5, −8)

b $2 + f(x)$:   A (−10, 2), B (1, 2), C (5, −1)

5 a $f(2x)$:   A (−5, 0), B $\left(\dfrac{1}{2}, 0\right)$, C (2.5, −3)

b $f(-x)$:   A (10, 0), B (−1, 0), C (−5, −3)

c $f(\dfrac{1}{2}x)$:   A (−20, 0), B (2, 0), C (10, −3)

6

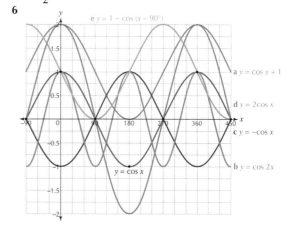

2.12 Changing the subject of a formula

1 a $r = \frac{1}{3}(f^2 + e)$ **b** $r = \sqrt{\frac{3V}{\pi h}}$

  c $r = \frac{gT^2}{4\pi^2}$ or $g\left(\frac{T}{2\pi}\right)^2$

2 a $x = \frac{7 - y}{2t}$ **b** $x = \frac{4y + 3}{2}$ **c** $x = \frac{bt - ar}{a - b}$

3 a $x = \frac{a}{b^2 - 3}x$ **b** $r = \sqrt{\frac{t - b}{a + c}}$ **c** $x = \frac{acd}{b + ac}$

4 a $r = \frac{y^2 - 1}{x}$ **b** $y = \sqrt{xr + 1}$

2.13 Solving simultaneous equations: one linear, one non-linear

1 a $x = 4$, $y = 8$ and $x = -1$, $y = 3$

  b $x = 2$, $y = 8$ and $x = -1$, $y = 2$

2 $x = 4$, $y = 8$ and $x = -2$, $y = 20$

3 Line 4 should say $0 = x^2 + 4x + 3$

  Line 5 $(x + 3)(x + 1) = 0$ so $x = -1$, $x = -3$

4 Intersect at $(5, -2)$ and $(2, -5)$; length of AB $= 3\sqrt{2}$

5 Error in factorisation line 8

  $2(x + 3)(x - 2)$ when $x = -3$, $y = -2$ and
  when $x = 2$, $y = 3$.

6 a $x = -\frac{4}{3}$, $-y = -2$

  b Sketch 2 is correct, as the line touches the curve
  just once. The line is a tangent to the curve.

2.14 Solving quadratic equations

1 $(2x - 3)(x + 5) = 0$; $x = -1.5$, $x = -5$

2 $(4x + 1)(3x - 2) = 0$; $x = -0.25$, $x = \frac{2}{3}$

3 $(3x + 7)(2x - 8) = 0$; $x = -\frac{7}{3}$, $x = 4$

4 Line 7: should say $x = -\frac{1}{2}$ or $x = -3$

5 $(3x + 7)(3x - 4) = 0$; $x = -\frac{7}{3}$, $x = \frac{4}{3}$

6 $x = 4$ cm

7 $(9x + 4)(x - 3) = 0$; $x = -\frac{4}{9}$, $x = 3$

2.15 Solving quadratic equations:

using $x = \frac{-b \pm \sqrt{b^2 - 4ac}}{2a}$

1 a $x = 1.16$, $x = -1.56$ **b** $x = 4.19$, $x = -1.19$

2 $\frac{2 \pm \sqrt{10}}{2}$

3 $\frac{1 \pm \sqrt{13}}{3}$

2.16 Completing the square

1 a $(x + 2)^2 - 10$ **b** $(x + 10)^2 - 101$

  c $\left(x + 2\frac{1}{2}\right)^2 - 6\frac{3}{4}$

2 a $x = 4 \pm \sqrt{3}$ **b** $\frac{-3 \pm \sqrt{41}}{2}$

3 a $2(x - 1.5)^2 - 5.5$; $(1.5, -5.5)$ **b** $y \geqslant -5.5$

  c $\frac{3 \pm \sqrt{11}}{2}$ **d** $y = -1$

  e

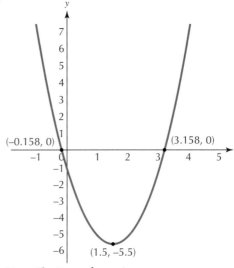

4 a $3(x - 1)^2 + 7$ **b** $x = 1$

  c Coordinates of minimum point are $(1, 7)$ so curve
  lies above the x axis and does not cross the x axis.

5 a $y = x^2 + 2x + 3 = (x + 1)^2 + 2$ so min value of $y = 2$.

  b $(x + 1)^2 \geqslant 0$ so $(x + 1)^2 + 2$ is always positive and
  $y \geqslant 2$.

  As graph does not cross x axis there are no real
  roots.

2.17 Solving inequalities

1 a $E = 12x$ **b** $A = 4\sqrt{3}x^2$ **c** $\frac{\sqrt{3}}{3}$

2 a Area A $= \frac{4x^2\sqrt{3}}{3}$, area B $= 4x^2$ and hence for any
  value of x, area A $<$ area B.

  b $x = \sqrt{3}$ **c** $x < \sqrt{3} + \sqrt{6}$

3 $\{x: x \leqslant -3 \cup x \geqslant 5\}$

4 $\{x: x < -1 \cup x > 3.5\}$

5 $\left\{x: -\frac{5}{3} \leqslant x \leqslant \frac{2}{3}\right\}$

2.18 Simplifying algebraic fractions

1 a $x + 7$ **b** $2x$ **c** $\dfrac{x-4}{x+3}$ **d** $\dfrac{1}{x+4}$

e $\dfrac{x-2}{3x-2}$ **f** $\dfrac{5(x-1)}{x+2}$

2.19 Simplifying algebraic fractions (addition and subtraction)

1 a $\dfrac{2c+13}{5}$ **b** $\dfrac{3d+7e}{de}$

2 $\dfrac{2(8x-11)}{(x+3)(x-4)}$ or $\dfrac{16x-22}{(x+3)(x-4)}$

3 a $\dfrac{1-x}{(x-3)(x-5)}$ **b** $\dfrac{10x-48}{(x-5)^2}$

c $\dfrac{5x-9}{(x+9)(x-9)}$

4 $\dfrac{9(x+3)}{5}$

5 $p = -4$, $q = -20$

2.20 Simplifying algebraic fractions (multiplication and division)

1 a $\dfrac{y}{5}$ **b** $\dfrac{5x^2}{y^5}$ **c** $5a$ **d** $5a$

2 a $\dfrac{5(x-3)}{3(x+5)}$ **b** $\dfrac{(t-4)}{4}$ **c** $\dfrac{x(x+3)}{x^2+3}$

3 a $\dfrac{3(x+4)}{x-2}$ **b** $\dfrac{x(x-4)}{(3x-4)^2}$

2.21 Solving equations with algebraic fractions

1 $x = 5.6$ **2** $x = -37$ **3** $x = -11\frac{1}{6}$ **4** $x = 46$

5 $x = 7$ **6** $x = 32.5$ **7** $x = 6.5$

2.22 Identities and proof

1

Position	1	2	3	4	5	n	$n+1$
Term	1	3	6	10	15		
	$\dfrac{1\times 2}{2}$	$\dfrac{2\times 3}{2}$	$\dfrac{3\times 4}{2}$	$\dfrac{4\times 5}{2}$	$\dfrac{5\times 6}{2}$	$\dfrac{n\times(n+1)}{2}$	$\dfrac{(n+1)\times(n+2)}{2}$

$\dfrac{n\times(n+1)}{2} + \dfrac{(n+1)\times(n+2)}{2} = \dfrac{(n+1)}{2}[n+n+2]$

$= \dfrac{(n+1)}{2} \times \dfrac{2(n+1)}{1}$

$= (n+1)^2$ the $(n+1)$th square number

2 Let consecutive odd numbers be $2n+1$ and $2n+3$

$2n+1+2n+3 = 4n+4 = 4(n+1)$ so a multiple of 4

3 Let first integer be n; then next consecutive number is $n+1$

$(n+1)^2 - n^2 = n^2 + 2n + 1 - n^2 = 2n+1 = n + (n+1)$ the sum of the two integers

4 $(2x-3)^3 \equiv (2x-3)(2x-3)^2 \equiv (2x-3)(4x^2 - 12x + 9)$
$= 2x(4x^2 - 12x + 9) - 3(4x^2 - 12x + 9)$

$(2x-3)^3 \equiv 8x^3 - 24x^2 + 18x - 12x^2 + 36x - 27$
$\equiv 8x^3 - 36x^2 + 54x - 27$

5 $\dfrac{1}{x^2+x} - \dfrac{1}{x^2-2x} \equiv \dfrac{1}{x(x+1)} - \dfrac{1}{x(x-2)}$

$\dfrac{1}{x(x+1)} - \dfrac{1}{x(x-2)} = \dfrac{(x-2)-(x+1)}{x(x+1)(x-2)}$

$= \dfrac{x-2-x-1}{x(x+1)(x-2)} = \dfrac{-3}{x(x+1)(x-2)}$

$A = -3$

6 $(2n+1)^3 - (2n-1)^3$
$= 8n^3 + 12n^2 + 6n + 1 - (8n^3 - 12n^2 + 6n - 1)$
$= 24n^2 + 2$ $a = 24$, $b = 2$

2.23 Sequences and iteration

1 $9n - 21$

2 a $\dfrac{13}{6}$ **b** $\dfrac{2n+1}{n}$ **c** $\dfrac{9}{2}$

3 General term $= \dfrac{\sqrt{n+1}}{n}$; 12th term $= \dfrac{\sqrt{13}}{12}$

4 $0, 3, 8, 15, 24$

5 a $21, 34$ **b** $3+5+8+13+21+34 = 4 \times 21 = 84$

6 a $5, 12, 21, 32, 45$

b 21

7 a 2^{n-1} **b** 2^{51}

8 a $(n+1)(n+2)$ or $n^2 + 3n + 2$

b 420 **c** 43

9 $2(8)^{-2} + 3(8) - 25 = -0.96875$

$2(9)^{-2} + 3(9) - 25 = 2.02469$

Change in sign, therefore root exists between 8 and 9

10 a $x^3 - 8x = 25$ gives $x^3 - 8x - 25 = 0$
Let $f(x) = x^3 - 8x - 25$

$f(3) = -22$ $f(4) = 7$ sign change implies root between 3 and 4

b $x^3 - 8x = 25$ gives $x^3 = 8x + 25$ so $x = \sqrt[3]{8x + 25}$

c Using $x_{n+1} = \sqrt[3]{8x_n + 25}$ with $x_0 = 3.5$

$x_1 = 3.756285...$

$x_2 = 3.804111...$

$x_3 = 3.812903...$

$x_4 = 3.814515...$

$x_5 = 3.814811...$

Solution is 3.815 to 3 decimal places.

11 a $x_1 = -4.296$, $x_2 = -4.325$, $x_3 = -4.321$ (to 3 decimal places)

b x_1, x_2 and x_3 are the first three solutions of the iterative form of the equation $x^3 + 4x^2 + 6 = 0$ and are estimates for one of the roots of this equation (solution -4.321 to 3 decimal places.)

12 $p + q = 9$, $2p + 3q = 23$, solving simultaneously gives
$p = 4$, $q = 5$.

13 a $a + 2b$, $2a + 3b$, $3a + 5b$

b $a + b + a + b + a + 2b + 2a + 3b + 3a + 5b = 8a + 12b$

$$4 \times (2a + 3b) = 8a + 12b$$

so the sum of the first 6 terms = $4 \times$ 5th term

ANSWERS TO CHAPTER 3: RATIO, PROPORTION AND CHANGE

3.1 Ratios, fractions and percentages

1 a $n = 12$ **b** $n = 2\sqrt{5}$

2 a $5 : 4$ **b i** $\frac{6}{13}$ **ii** \$514.57

3 a $30 : 42 : 25$ **b** €840   **c** €121.80

d The sum of the parts of the ratio are equal to 97.

4 a $212 : 351 : 330 : 262$ **b** 190 680 000 **c** 54.971 million

5 $y = \dfrac{x(p - 1)}{2 + p}$

6 a $y = \dfrac{4x}{3}$ **b** $9 : 10$

7 a $y = \dfrac{5x}{6}$ **b** $4 : 3$

8 a £1 599 338   **b** 43.8%

9 a 300g   **b** $12 : 32 : 41 : 48$

10

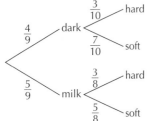

dark, soft $\dfrac{4}{9} \times \dfrac{7}{10} = \dfrac{28}{90}$

milk, soft $\dfrac{5}{9} \times \dfrac{5}{8} = \dfrac{25}{72}$

Fraction with soft centres $= \dfrac{28}{90} + \dfrac{25}{72} = \dfrac{79}{120}$

11 a £1200   **b** 3.500%

12 £1.10

3.2 Direct and inverse proportion

1 a $y \propto \dfrac{1}{x}$ **b** $y \propto x$ **c** $y \propto x^2$

2 a $y = \dfrac{x}{4}$ **b** 12   **c** 11

3 a 10   **b** 4

4 a i 153.86   **ii** 8.45

b $V = 7776\pi$ cm³

5 a 10 minutes 40 seconds or $10\frac{2}{3}$ minutes

b 7 minutes

6 a Table B, missing value is $y = 5$

b Table A, missing value is $y = 4.5$

c Table C, missing value is $y = 2.5$

7 2.5 cm

8

a	2	4	1	10
b	4	2	8	0.8

9 a 9.6 days   **b** 32 bricklayers

3.3 Compound measure

1 a 36 min   **b** 2 h 15 min

c 71 s   **d** 1 h 12 m

2 a 64.8 km/h   **b** 201 km/h

c 1.8 km/h   **d** 2 km/h

3 a 76 km   **b** 427 km

c 54 km   **d** 4 km

4 a 360 km   **b** 77 km/h

5 a $a = \dfrac{5}{6}$ m/s   **b** $s = 15$ m

6 0.864 g/cm²

7 93.89g (4 sf)

8 a 112.128 g   **b** 17.7 mm × 42.5 mm × 14.2 mm

9 a 321 428 571.4 N/m²   **b** 1.8×10^{-6} m²

10 38.25 N

11 a $s = \dfrac{3u^2}{4}$ m   **b** $u = 2\sqrt{15}$ m/s

12 a 0.204 kg   **b** 284.09 g   **c** 8.7268 g

3.4 Ratios of length, area and volume

1 $2 : 7 : 9$

2 85.7%

3 $h : b = 2 : 1$

4 a volume P : volume Q $= 6xyz : 12xyz = 1 : 2$

b volume P : volume Q $= 6xyz : 12xyz = 1 : 2$

Hence volume of Q = $2 \times$ volume of Q

5 a i 28 cm²   **ii** 42 cm²

b i base $= \dfrac{7\sqrt{10}}{5}$, height $= 2\sqrt{10}$

6 a i base $= \dfrac{21\sqrt{15}}{10} = \dfrac{7\sqrt{15}}{5}$, height $\dfrac{7\sqrt{15}}{15} = 2\sqrt{15}$ **c** $\dfrac{7\sqrt{6}}{6}$

7 a 474.4 cm² (1 dp)   **b** $T : H = 475 : 699$

8 a i $a^2 : b^2$ **ii** $a^3 : b^3$

b i $6a : 5b$ **ii** $36a^2 : 25b^2$ **iii** $216a^3 : 125b^3$

ANSWERS TO CHAPTER 4: GEOMETRY AND MEASURES

4.1 Arcs and sectors

1 a 5.24 cm   **b** 9.77 cm   **c** 15.7 cm

2 a 8π **b** $\dfrac{63}{2}\pi$ or 31.5π

   c $\dfrac{216}{125}\pi$ or 1.728π

3 a 60°   **b** 12°   **c** 20°

4 a 11.49 m²   **b** 26

5 42.5°

6 19.3 cm²

7 119 cm²

8 63.2%

9 145 m²

4.2 Surface area and volume

1 110.88π cm²

2 3524.5 cm² (1 dp)

3 550π

4 275π

5 170 cm³

6 1699 g

7 a 25 525 kg

   b £3074 (incl. base)   £2493 (excl. base)

8 609.375π cm³

4.3 Similarity

1 $h = 31.25$ cm

2 a 123.75 cm²   **b** 533.33 g

3 94 770 cm³

4 a $\dfrac{2\sqrt{21}}{3}$ cm or 3.05 cm (3 sf)   **b** 6.92 cm²

5 5.26 cm

6 a $x = \sqrt{6}$ cm, therefore perimeter $= 8\sqrt{6}$ cm

   b $16\sqrt{3}$ cm

7 11250 cm³

8 a 8.91 cm   **b** 78.5 cm³

9 a 9 cm   **b** 750π cm³

10 1824π cm³

11 Using triangle PQR similar to triangle PST gives $h = 3$ cm; using triangle PQR similar to triangle PTS gives $h = 24\dfrac{1}{3}$ cm.

4.4 Trigonometry

1 a 3039 m   **b** 547 km/h

2 RS = 14.8 cm

3 PR = 15.5 cm

4

	sin	cos	tan
30°	$\dfrac{1}{2}$	$\dfrac{\sqrt{3}}{2}$	$\dfrac{\sqrt{3}}{3}$
45°	$\dfrac{\sqrt{2}}{2}$	$\dfrac{\sqrt{2}}{2}$	1
60°	$\dfrac{\sqrt{3}}{2}$	$\dfrac{1}{2}$	$\sqrt{3}$
90°	1	0	not defined

5 13.0°

6 a 13.8 cm   **b** 18.4°   **c** 12.6°

7 74.8 m

8 67.0°

9 a $32 - 25 = 7$ cm   **b** 56.4°

10 Using trigonometry on the right angled triangle $\cos\theta = \dfrac{\text{adjacent}}{\text{hypotenuse}}$.

If angle $\theta = 60°$ then the base of the triangle would be equal to half of the hypotenuse as $\cos 60 = \dfrac{1}{2}$

The base of this triangle is equal to

$$\sqrt{\left(\dfrac{2\sqrt{5}}{3}\right)} - \sqrt{\left(\dfrac{\sqrt{15}}{3}\right)^2} = \sqrt{\dfrac{20}{9}} - \sqrt{\dfrac{15}{9}} = \sqrt{\dfrac{5}{9}}$$

$\sqrt{\dfrac{5}{9}} = \dfrac{\sqrt{5}}{3}$ and hence $2 \times \dfrac{\sqrt{5}}{3} = \dfrac{2\sqrt{5}}{3}$; therefore $\cos\theta = \dfrac{1}{2}$ and hence 60°.

4.5 Sine rule and cosine rule

1 a 4.58 cm   **b** 82.1°

2 20.9 km

3 17 cm

4 a 132.4 km   **b** 314°

4.6 Areas of triangles

1 153 cm²

2 2650 m²

3 84 m²

4 $x = 4.15$ cm

5 10 708 m²

6 10 cm²

7 a 4763 m² (4sf)   **b** 34% (2sf)

4.7 Congruent triangles

1 AB = CD (opposite sides of a parallelogram), BC = DA (opposite sides of a parallelogram), AC is common, so triangle ABC is congruent to triangle CDA (SSS).

Or: ∠BAC = ∠ACD (alternate angles), ∠BCA = ∠CAD (alternate angles), AC is common, so triangle ABC is congruent to triangle CDA (ASA).

2 AB = DE (given), ∠ABC = ∠EDC (alternate angles), ∠BAC = ∠DEC (alternate angles), so triangle ABC is congruent to triangle EDC (ASA).

3 AB = AD (given), BC = DC (given), AC is common, so triangle ABC is congruent to triangle ADC (SSS), therefore ∠ABC = ∠ADC.

4 AB = CD (sides of a regular pentagon), BC = DE (sides of a regular pentagon), ∠ABC = ∠CDE (interior angles of a regular pentagon), so triangle ABC is congruent to triangle CDE (SAS).

5 a Shape is made of six identical triangles each with an area of $25\sqrt{3}$ hence total area is $150\sqrt{3}$.

b The area of one of the equilateral triangles is $\frac{\sqrt{3}}{4}x^2$, when multiplied by 6 this gives $\frac{3\sqrt{3}}{2}x^2$.

6 a

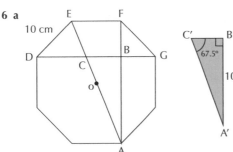

DG ∥ EF, exterior angles = 45°

∴ ∠BFG = ∠FGB = 45°

BF = $5\sqrt{2}$ (Pythagoras)

AF = $10\sqrt{2} + 10$ cm

AB = $5\sqrt{2} + 10$ cm

EF : CB = AF : AB

10 : CB = $10 + 10\sqrt{2}$: $10 + \sqrt{5}$

$\frac{CB}{10} = \frac{10(10 + 5\sqrt{2})}{10 + 10\sqrt{2}}$

CB = $5\sqrt{2}$ ∠DEF = 135°

AE bisects DEF ∴ ∠AEF = 67.5°

BA = $10 + 5\sqrt{2}$

Hence ∠ACB = 67.5°

b Area ΔABC = $\frac{(10 + 5\sqrt{2})(5\sqrt{2})}{2}$ = $25\sqrt{2} + 25$

= $25\sqrt{2} + 25 = 60.63$ (2 dp)

4.8 Circle theorems

1 a $a = 78°$ (angle at the centre is twice the angle at the circumference, when subtended by the same arc)

b $b = 66°$ (angle at the centre is twice the angle at the circumference, when subtended by the same arc)

c $c = 41°$ (angles at the circumference are equal, when subtended by the same arc)

d $d = 67°$ (angles at the circumference are equal, when subtended by the same arc)

e $e = 90°$ (angle in a semicircle)

f $f = 100°$ (sum of opposite angles of a cyclic quadrilateral is 180°)

g $g = 20°$ (obtuse angle at O = 160°, radii meet the tangents at 90°, angle sum of quadrilateral is 360°)

h $h = 50°$ (angle in the alternate segment)

i $i = 10°$ (angle in the alternate segment gives two angles of 85°, angle sum of triangle is 180°)

j $j = 72°$ (supplementary angle to 115° is 65°, third angle in triangle is 72°, which is equal to j (as opposite angles of cyclic quadrilateral, supplementary angles)

k $k = 58°$ (angle in the alternate segment), $l = 58°$ (base angles of isosceles triangle), $m = 76°$ (angle in the alternate segment), $n = 104°$ (opposite angles of cyclic quadrilateral)

2 Given a diameter, the angle at the centre is 180° since it is a straight line.

The angle at the circumference is half the angle at the centre.

So the angle in the semicircle is 90°.

3 ABCD is a cyclic quadrilateral where opposite angles sum to 180° therefore ∠BAD = 180°− θ. Line DAE is 180°, therefore ∠BAE = 180° − (180° − θ) = θ.

4 a $x = 46°$ **b** $y = 22°$

5 Join the two points at the bottom to the centre, then use the fact that the angle at the circumference is half the angle at the centre, for both angles.

6

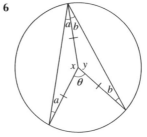

Add a radius to diagram

The two triangles are isoceles

$x = 180 - 2a$ (sum of angles in triangle)

$y = 180 - 2b$ (sum of angles in triangle)

so $x + y = 360 - (2a + 2b)$

$\theta + x + y = 360°$ (angles at a point)

$\theta = 360 - (x + y)$

$= 360 - (360 - (2a + 2b))$

$= 2a + 2b = 2(a + b)$

Angle at centre $= 2(a + b)$

Angle at circumferences $= a + b$

Therefore, the angle subtended by the arc at the centre of the circle is twice the angle subtended by the arc at the circumference.

4.9 Enlargement

1

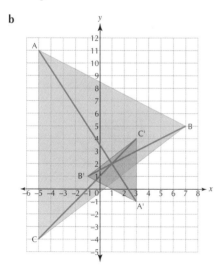

2 a $-\dfrac{4}{3}$

b

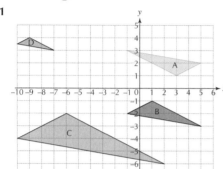

c (1, 2)

d Enlargement, scale factor 3, centre (1, 2)

3 a Scale factor 3

b Centre of enlargement (0, −2); scale factor 2

4.10 Vectors

1 a Any two of the single horizontal line segments, e.g. $\overrightarrow{DE}$, $\overrightarrow{JK}$

b Any two of the single sloping line segments, e.g. $\overrightarrow{DH}$, $\overrightarrow{NS}$

c Any two of the single horizontal line segments reversed, e.g. $\overrightarrow{ED}$, $\overrightarrow{KJ}$

d Any two of the single sloping line segments reversed, e.g. $\overrightarrow{HD}$, $\overrightarrow{SN}$

e $\overrightarrow{OC} = 3\mathbf{a}$ **f** $\overrightarrow{FH} = \mathbf{b} - 2\mathbf{a}$ **g** $\overrightarrow{OT} = 3\mathbf{a} + 4\mathbf{b}$

h $\overrightarrow{AN} = \mathbf{a} + 3\mathbf{b}$ **I** $\overrightarrow{IK} = 2\mathbf{a}$ **j** $\overrightarrow{NC} = \mathbf{a} - 3\mathbf{b}$

2

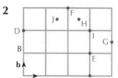

a $\overrightarrow{OC} = 3\mathbf{a}$ **b** $\overrightarrow{OD} = 2\mathbf{b}$

c $\overrightarrow{OE} = 3\mathbf{a} + \mathbf{b}$ **d** $\overrightarrow{OF} = 2\mathbf{a} + 3\mathbf{b}$

e $\overrightarrow{OG} = 4\mathbf{a} + \dfrac{3}{2}\mathbf{b}$ **f** $\overrightarrow{OH} = \dfrac{5}{2}(\mathbf{a} + \mathbf{b})$

g $\overrightarrow{IO} = -3\mathbf{a} - 2\mathbf{b}$ **h** $\overrightarrow{JO} = -\dfrac{3}{2}\mathbf{a} - \dfrac{5}{2}\mathbf{b}$

3 a $\overrightarrow{AB} = \mathbf{b} - \mathbf{a}$ **b** $\overrightarrow{AM} = \dfrac{1}{2}(\mathbf{b} - \mathbf{a})$

c $\overrightarrow{BA} = \mathbf{a} - \mathbf{b}$ **e** $\overrightarrow{BM} = \dfrac{1}{2}(\mathbf{a} - \mathbf{b})$

f $\overrightarrow{OM} = \dfrac{1}{2}(\mathbf{a} + \mathbf{b})$ **g** $\overrightarrow{MO} = -\dfrac{1}{2}(\mathbf{a} + \mathbf{b})$

4 a $\overrightarrow{AB} = 2(\mathbf{b} - \mathbf{a})$ **b** $\overrightarrow{DC} = 2\mathbf{b}$

c $\overrightarrow{FE} = -2\mathbf{a}$ **d** $\overrightarrow{EM} = 4\mathbf{b} - \mathbf{a}$

5 a $\dfrac{2}{5}\overline{a} + \dfrac{3}{5}\overline{b} = \overrightarrow{OC}$ **b** $\dfrac{2}{5}\overline{a}$

6 Let M_1 = midpoint of $\overrightarrow{AC}$ and let M_2 = midpoint $\overrightarrow{DB}$

From this, $\dfrac{1}{2}\overrightarrow{AC} = AM_1$ and $\dfrac{1}{2}\overrightarrow{DB} = DM_2$

$\dfrac{1}{2}\overrightarrow{AC} = \dfrac{1}{2}\overrightarrow{AD} + \dfrac{1}{2}\overrightarrow{BC} + \dfrac{1}{2}\overrightarrow{DB}$

$\dfrac{1}{2}\overrightarrow{AC} = \dfrac{1}{2}\overrightarrow{AB} + \dfrac{1}{2}\overrightarrow{BC}$ but also $\dfrac{1}{2}(\overrightarrow{AD} + \overrightarrow{DB} + \overrightarrow{BC}) = \dfrac{1}{2}\overrightarrow{AC}$

Hence M_1 and M_2 are the same point (m).

7 $\overrightarrow{AB} + \overrightarrow{BC} = \overrightarrow{AC}$

$\overrightarrow{PB} = \dfrac{1}{2}\overrightarrow{AB}$ $\overrightarrow{BQ} = \dfrac{1}{2}\overrightarrow{BC}$

$\Rightarrow \dfrac{1}{2}(\overrightarrow{AB} + \overrightarrow{BC}) = \dfrac{1}{2}\overrightarrow{AC}$

$\therefore \overrightarrow{PB} + \overrightarrow{BQ} = \overrightarrow{PC} = \dfrac{1}{2}\overrightarrow{AC}$

$\overrightarrow{AD} + \overrightarrow{DC} = \overrightarrow{AC} \Rightarrow \dfrac{1}{2}(\overrightarrow{AD} + \overrightarrow{DC}) = \dfrac{1}{2}\overrightarrow{AC}$

$\overrightarrow{SD} = \dfrac{1}{2}\overrightarrow{AD}$ $\overrightarrow{DR} = \dfrac{1}{2}\overrightarrow{DC}$

$\therefore \dfrac{1}{2}\overrightarrow{AD} + \dfrac{1}{2}\overrightarrow{DC} = \overrightarrow{SR}$ $\therefore \overrightarrow{SR} = \dfrac{1}{2}\overrightarrow{AC}$

Hence $\therefore \overrightarrow{PQ} = \overrightarrow{SR}$

(The same logic can be applied to show that $\overrightarrow{QR} = \overrightarrow{PS}$)

8 $\overrightarrow{QR} = 4\mathbf{p} - 3\mathbf{q} - 2\mathbf{p} - \mathbf{q} = 2\mathbf{p} - 4\mathbf{q}$

$\overrightarrow{QS} = 4\mathbf{p} - 3\mathbf{q} + 2\mathbf{p} - 8\mathbf{q} = 6\mathbf{p} - 11\mathbf{q}$

$\overrightarrow{QS} \neq k\overrightarrow{QR}$ so QRS is not a straight line

9 $k = 5$

ANSWERS TO CHAPTER 5: STATISTICS AND PROBABILITY

5.1 Cumulative frequency graphs and box plots

1 a

Time, t (mins)	Cumulative frequency
$0 \le t < 5$	18
$0 \le t < 10$	25
$0 \le t < 15$	60
$0 \le t < 20$	82
$0 \le t < 25$	93
$0 \le t < 30$	100

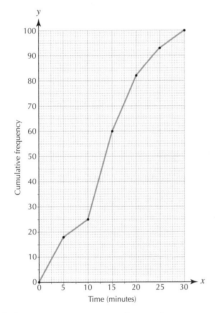

b i 13.5 ± 0.5 minutes **ii** 10 minutes

iii 18.5 ± 0.5 minutes **iv** 8.5 ± 0.5 minutes

c 38 ± 1 **d** 14 ± 1 **e** 38 ± 2

f The median for medical practice B, 12.5 mins, is less than the median for medical practice A, 13.5 mins, which implies the waiting times for B are on average less than the waiting times for A.

The IQR for medical practice A is the same as the IQR for medical practice B, which implies the waiting times at A and B are equally spread.

g The range for medical practice B is 32 − 2 = 30 mins, but as you do not know the exact values for the times in medical practice A, you cannot work out the range in times for this practice.

2 a 7 g **b** 29 **c** 11.25% **d** $\frac{1}{8}$

e The sample of 10 from farm B is very small and may not be representative. It is compared with the sample of 80 from farm A and may not form a valid comparison. Although the LQ and UQ values are higher for farm B, the median is lower so the comparison is inconclusive and a larger sample is needed. The use of the word 'bigger' could imply the dimensions of the eggs rather than weight, so the statement is not clear.

3 a The points on a cumulative frequency graph should be joined with a smooth curve.

b Probability $= \frac{80}{200} \times 100 = 40\%$. This is less than the claim made on the seed packet.

5.2 Histograms

1 a

Height, h (cm)	$100 < h \le 110$	$110 < h \le 125$	$125 < h \le 135$	$135 < h \le 150$	$150 < h \le 155$
Class width	10	15	10	15	5
Frequency	8	33	37	18	4
Frequency density	0.8	2.2	3.7	1.2	0.8

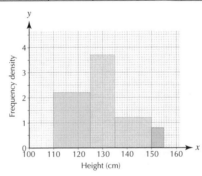

b i 84 (see histogram)

ii Position of median = 50.5, 8 + 33 = 41, median is x into interval $125 < h \le 135$, where $x = (50.5 - 41) \div 3.7 = 2.567$

$125 + 2.567 \approx 127.5$ cm

iii 16.5 cm

c 127.025 cm

2 a

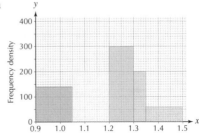

b i 69 **ii** 1.2 m **iii** 0.21 m

c 1.178 m

3 a 9 **b** 3 or 4

4 a

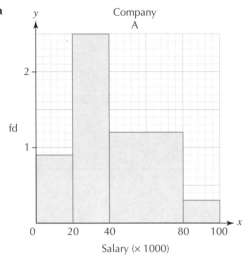

Company A

b 76

c Estimates for summary statistics

	Lower quartile	Median	Upper quartile	IQR
Company A	£25 400	£38 400	£60 800	£35 400
Company B	£24 600	£45 333	£63 000	£38 400

The salaries were higher on average at Company B than Company A. Difference in estimate for median is £7333.

The salaries at Company B were more spread at Company B than at Company A. There is a difference of £3000 in the estimate for the interquartile range for the two companies.

5.3 Sampling

1 a Method **iii** would give a random sample, as all students are equally likely to be chosen.

b Reasons: Method **i** restricts the choice to Year 8 students. Method **ii** restricts the choice to those students who are early for school.

2 a In a stratified sample the number selected from each group, or strata, is proportional to the group size, so that each strata is represented in the sample.

b

Year group	Girls	Boys	Total
7	9	9	18
8	9	9	18
9	10	11	21
10	10	11	21
11	10	12	22
Total	48	52	100

3

Country	Students	Sample size
Belgium	30	3
France	50	4
Germany	72	6
Luxembourg	12	1
Netherlands	40	3
Italy	84	7

4 $\frac{30}{N} = \frac{6}{40}$ $N = 200$

5.4 Sample space diagrams and experimental probability

1 a

H	4	8	16	20
T	2	4	8	10

b $\frac{3}{8}$ **c** 7

2 a $\frac{5}{12}$ **b** $\frac{25}{144}$ **c** 216

d It is easier to win in game 1 as the probability is $\frac{5}{12}$. The second game gives a smaller probability of $\frac{3}{8}$.

3 a i $\frac{18}{43}$ **ii** $\frac{2}{5}$ **b i** $\frac{2}{25}$ **ii** $\frac{5}{43}$ **c** $\frac{18}{43}$

5.5 Conditional probability and tree diagrams

1 a $\frac{1}{11}$ **b** $\frac{5}{22}$ **c** $\frac{1}{66}$ **d** $\frac{1}{33}$

2

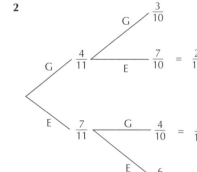

$\frac{56}{110} = 50.9\%$

3 P(3 vowels no replacement) = $\frac{4}{7} \times \frac{2}{6} \times \frac{2}{5} = \frac{4}{35}$ and

P(2 consonants and 1 vowel no replacement)

= $\frac{3}{7} \times \frac{2}{6} \times \frac{4}{5} = \frac{4}{35}$

4 a i $\frac{1}{10}$ **ii** $\frac{17}{60}$ **b** 17 : 43

   c $\frac{1}{66}$

5 a TABLE A OUTCOMES

	2	5	−10
2	x	7	−8
5	7	x	−5
−10	−8	−5	x

b TABLE B CARD 1 OUTCOMES

	−2	−5	10
7	9	12	−3
7	9	12	−3
−5	−3	0	−15
−5	−3	0	−15
−8	−6	−3	−18
−8	−6	−3	−18

TABLE B CARDS 2 OUTCOMES

	2	−5	10
9	x	−45	90
9	x	−45	90
−3	x	15	−30
−3	x	15	−30
−6	x	30	−60
−6	x	30	−60
12	24	x	120
12	24	x	120
0	0	x	0
0	0	x	0
−3	−6	x	−30
−3	−6	x	−30
−3	−6	15	x
−3	−6	15	x
−15	−30	75	x
−15	−30	75	x
−18	−36	90	x
−18	−36	90	x

36 outcomes

p(> 0) $\frac{16}{36} = \frac{4}{9}$

p(≤ 20) $\frac{24}{36} = \frac{2}{3}$

6 1 − P(wins no prizes)

= $\frac{356}{360} \times \frac{355}{359} \times \frac{354}{358} \times \frac{353}{357}$ = 1 − 0.956 = 0.044

5.6 Venn diagrams and mutually exclusive events

1 a

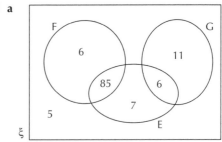

b i $\frac{13}{15}$ **ii** $\frac{29}{120}$ **iii** $\frac{49}{60}$ **iv** $\frac{17}{120}$

2 a

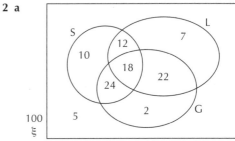

b i $\frac{7}{100}$ **ii** $\frac{1}{10}$ **iii** $\frac{1}{20}$ **iv** $\frac{29}{50}$

c $\frac{40}{66} = \frac{20}{33}$ **d** $\frac{30}{59}$

3 a

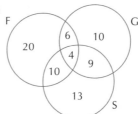

b 4

c i $\frac{4}{60} = \frac{1}{15}$ **ii** $\frac{47}{60}$ **iii** $\frac{32}{60} = \frac{8}{15}$ **d** $\frac{6}{21} = \frac{2}{7}$

1 a DE = 4.5 cm, Area ABED = 10.5 cm²   **b** 16 : 9

2 a 45 seconds

  b i 43.7 seconds   **ii** $t = \dfrac{1.385}{x}$ (in hours)

3 $y = \dfrac{x}{4}$

4 70 cm

5 a $61\dfrac{1}{3}\pi$ cm³   **b** 3.78 cm

6 a When $y = 0$, $10x - 5$ must $= $ zero, so $x = 0.5$.

  b If x is $\dfrac{4}{3}$, then $\sqrt{16 - 9\left(\dfrac{4}{3}\right)^2} = 0$, but you cannot

    divide by zero.

  c $-\dfrac{4}{3}$

7 a $1 + \sqrt{2}$ cm

  b ∠BAH = 135°; ∠BAH = 90°; ∠CBG = 135 − 90 = 45°
    since ∠BAH + ∠CBG = 180°; AH and BG are parallel

8 1 litre

9 120 cm²

10 (10, 5), 30 units²

11 (18, 15)

12 155.5 + 16.5 + 16.5 = 188.5 < 189.5, will not overflow.

13 Radius = 8 cm, volume = 128π cm³, mass = 256π g

14 60°

15 a Side of square: long part = x, short part = y

    Area of square $= (x + y)^2 = x^2 + 2xy + y^2$

    Using Pythagoras' theorem: $x^2 = \dfrac{a^2}{2}$, $x = \dfrac{a}{\sqrt{2}}$

    $y^2 = \dfrac{b^2}{2}$, $y = \dfrac{b}{\sqrt{2}}$

    Area of square $= \dfrac{a^2}{2} + 2 \times \dfrac{a}{\sqrt{2}} \times \dfrac{b}{\sqrt{2}} + \dfrac{b^2}{2}$

    $= \dfrac{a^2}{2} + ab + \dfrac{b^2}{2}$

    $= \dfrac{1}{2}\left(a^2 + 2ab + b^2\right)$

    $= \dfrac{1}{2}\left(a + b\right)^2$

  b $\tan \theta = \dfrac{DE}{EF} = \dfrac{1}{4}$

    $\therefore DE = \dfrac{1}{4}EF$ and thus $4DE = EF$

    Let $x = DE$, $\therefore 4x = EF$

    Using Pythagoras' theorem: $x^2 + \left(4x\right)^2 = \left(3\sqrt{17}\right)^2$

    $x^2 + 16x^2 = 17x^2 = 9 \times 17$

    $\therefore x^2 = 9$ and $x = 3$ cm

    So DE is 3 cm and EF is 12 cm, and hence the area
    of the square (EF²) is 144 cm².

16 a $\dfrac{7}{\tan 27} = BC$. BC is in the ratio 3 : 2

    $\therefore \dfrac{3}{5} \times \dfrac{7}{\tan 27}$ and $\dfrac{2}{5} \times \dfrac{7}{\tan 27}$

    $\left(\therefore BC = \dfrac{21}{5\tan 27} + \dfrac{14}{5\tan 27} = \dfrac{35}{5\tan 27}\right)$

  b 13.3°

17 Split into three triangles. Area CAB = $25\sqrt{3}$, area
    CDE = $30\sqrt{3}$, area ACE = $10\sqrt{15}$.

18 a $3x^2 - 8x + 8 = 0$

  b There will be no solution since the number
    inside the square root sign is negative (−32).

19 a The minimum number of tiles is 448.

  b She might need 72 more tiles.

20 Small = 6.56 inches² per £, big = 7.01 inches² per £,
    so big is better value.

21 a 3000 cm³   **b** 11 200 cm²

22 $1000 - 300x + 30x^2 - x^3$

20 a Let $\overrightarrow{AC} = a$ and $\overrightarrow{CE} = c$

    $\overrightarrow{AE} = a + c$ and $\overrightarrow{BD} = \dfrac{1}{2}a + \dfrac{1}{2}c = \dfrac{1}{2}(a + c)$

    Hence $\overrightarrow{AE}$ and $\overrightarrow{BD}$ are parallel with ratio of
    AE : BD = 2 : 1.

  b $\overrightarrow{CF} = -\dfrac{1}{2}a + \left(\dfrac{1}{3}\right)\left(\dfrac{1}{2}\right)(a + c) = -\dfrac{1}{2}a + \dfrac{1}{6}(a + c)$

    $= -\dfrac{1}{3}a + \dfrac{1}{6}c = \dfrac{1}{6}(-2a + c)$

    $\overrightarrow{FG} = -\left(\dfrac{1}{3}\right)\left(\dfrac{1}{2}\right)(a + c) - \dfrac{1}{2}a + \left(\dfrac{1}{3}\right)(a + c)$

    $= -\dfrac{1}{3}a + \dfrac{1}{6}c = \dfrac{1}{6}(-2a + c)$

    Hence $\overrightarrow{CF}$ and $\overrightarrow{FG}$ are parallel and have
    common point F and so the points C, F and G
    lie on a straight line.

24 a 4.8 cm   **b** 125 cm²   **c** 27

ANSWERS TO CHAPTER 7: SPOT THE ERRORS

1 a $\dfrac{5}{125} \times 100 = 4$ pence

  b i $\dfrac{43}{125} \times 40\,300 = £13\,863.20$ **ii** $\dfrac{40\,305}{1.215} = 33\,173$ litres

2 If true, then:

    $(2n + 2)^2 - (2n)^2 = 2 \times (2n + 2 + 2n)$

    $4n^2 + 4n + 4n + 4 - 4n^2 = 4n + 4 + 4n$

    $8n + 4 = 8n + 4$ (QED)

3 $p \propto r^2$

$p = kr^2$

$7.50 = k \times 1.5^2$

$k = 3\frac{1}{3}$

$p = 3\frac{1}{3}r^2$

$p = 3\frac{1}{3} \times 3^2$

$p = £30$

4 $a^2 + 8b = 121$

$a^2 - 16b = 1$

$24b = 120$

$b = 5$

$a^2 + 8 \times 5 = 121$

$a^2 + 40 = 121$

$a^2 = 81$

$a = 9$

So $\sqrt{a^2 - ab} = \sqrt{9^2 - 9 \times 5} = \sqrt{36} = 6$

5 $x^2 + y^2 = (x + 1)^2$

$x^2 + y^2 = x^2 + 2x + 1$

$y^2 = 2x + 1$

$2x + 1$ will be odd for any integer.

Only odd × odd gives an odd number, so y must be odd.

6 LHS $= \dfrac{\sqrt{20} + 10}{\sqrt{5}} \times \dfrac{\sqrt{5}}{\sqrt{5}}$

$= \dfrac{\sqrt{20}\sqrt{5} + 10\sqrt{5}}{\sqrt{5}\sqrt{5}}$

$= \dfrac{\sqrt{100} + 10\sqrt{5}}{5}$

$= \dfrac{10 + 10\sqrt{5}}{5}$

$= \dfrac{10\left(1 + \sqrt{5}\right)}{5}$

$= 2\left(1 + \sqrt{5}\right)$

$=$ RHS (Proved)

7

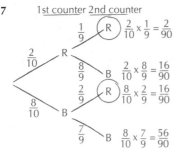

1st counter 2nd counter

$\frac{1}{9}$ R $\quad \frac{2}{10} \times \frac{1}{9} = \frac{2}{90}$

$\frac{2}{10}$ R

$\frac{8}{9}$ B $\quad \frac{2}{10} \times \frac{8}{9} = \frac{16}{90}$

$\frac{2}{9}$ R $\quad \frac{8}{10} \times \frac{2}{9} = \frac{16}{90}$

$\frac{8}{10}$ B

$\frac{7}{9}$ B $\quad \frac{8}{10} \times \frac{7}{9} = \frac{56}{90}$

Probability that the second ball is red

$\frac{2}{10} \times \frac{1}{9} + \frac{8}{10} \times \frac{2}{9} = \frac{2}{90} + \frac{16}{90} = \frac{18}{90} = \frac{1}{5}$

8 $2n$, $2n + 2$ and $2n + 4$ are three consecutive numbers

$(2n + 2n + 2 + 2n + 4)^2 = (6n + 6)^2$

$(6n + 6)^2 = 36n^2 + 72n + 36$

$= 36\,(n^2 + 2n + 1)$

$= 36\,(n + 1)^2$

$6084 = 36(n + 1)^2$

$\therefore 169 = (n + 1)^2$

$13 = n + 1$

$n = 12$ so integers are 24, 26 and 28

9 $x^2 + 4x + 3 = 0$ ③

$(x + 1)(x + 3) = 0$

$x = -1$ or $x = -3$

when $x = -1$, $y = 3$

when $x = -3$, $y = 7$

10 $x^2\sqrt{3} = 64\pi$

then

$x^2 = \dfrac{64\sqrt{3}\pi}{3}$

$x = \sqrt{\left(\dfrac{64\sqrt{3}\pi}{3}\right)}$

$x = 10.8$ cm (3 sf)

11

Marks, m	Class width	Frequency density	Frequency
$0 \leqslant m < 8$	8	0.5	4
$8 \leqslant m < 12$	4	0.75	3
$12 \leqslant m < 14$	2	2	4
$14 \leqslant m < 20$	6	1.5	9

median is $\dfrac{20 + 1}{2} = 10.5$ value. Lies in interval

$12 < m \leqslant 14$

median is $12 + x$, where $2 \times x = (10.5 - 4 - 3)$

i.e $2x = 3.5$ so $x = 1.75$

median $= 12 + 1.75 = 13.75$ marks

12 $\angle ACB = 180° - 128° = 52°$ (angles on a straight line)

Obtuse $\angle AOB = 2 \times ACB = 104°$ (angle at the centre is double the angle at the circumference when subtended from the same arc)

Reflex $\angle AOB = 360° - 104° = 256°$ (angles around a point sum to $360°$)

13 a 8 cm²   **b** 64 cm²   **c** 27 cm²

9 How to interpret the language of exam questions

If the question says:	The question means:
Calculate	Use a calculator or formal method. Your working should be written down.
Describe fully	In transformations: reflection – state equation of line of symmetry; translations – identify column vector; rotations – identify coordinates of centre of rotation, angle and direction of rotation, (clockwise or anticlockwise); enlargement – state scale factor and coordinates of centre of enlargement.
Draw an accurate drawing	Use a pair of compasses to draw lengths accurately and a protractor to measure and draw angles accurately (and use a sharp pencil).
Estimate	Commonly means round numbers to 1 significant figure to work out a calculation.
Expand	Multiply out brackets.
Expand and simplify	Multiply out brackets, then collect like terms. For example: Expand and simplify $2(y + 5) + 4(2y - 3)$ $$2(y + 5) + 4(2y - 3) = 2y + 10 + 8y - 12$$ $$= 10y - 2$$
Explain; Comment; Justify; Give a reason for your answer	Use words or a mathematical argument to explain an answer. A correct answer with no explanation may get zero marks. Examiners may want to see a keyword or fact, e.g. Susan's triangle has internal angles of 30°, 80° and 80°. Explain why this is wrong. (Answer: The internal angles of a triangle add up to 180° but these angles add up to 190°.)
You **must** show your working	You will be penalised and could get zero marks if you do not show your working.
Express x, in terms of …	Use given information to write an expression for x using only the letter(s) given, e.g. Express x in terms of z in the equation $12x = z + 3$ $$x = \frac{z + 3}{12}$$
Factorise	Identify a common factor to put outside a bracket (opposite of 'Expand'), e.g. Factorise $9x^2 + 6x$ $9x^2 + 6x = 3x\,(3x + 2)$
Factorise fully	Clue, that there may be more than one factor and/or e.g. factorise a quadratic.
Give a counter example	Give a numerical or geometrical example to disprove a statement; pick numbers that show a statement is untrue, e.g. Susan says a number is always smaller than its square. Counter example to show she is wrong: $\left(\frac{1}{2}\right)^2 = \frac{1}{2} \times \frac{1}{2} = \frac{1}{4}$
Give an exact value	Give your answer as a surd or a fraction – not as a rounded decimal. e.g. $\frac{1}{7} = 0.1428.....$ which is not exact. $\frac{1}{3} = 0.333....$ can be written as $0.\dot{3}$ but writing as $\frac{1}{3}$ is preferable
Give answer in terms of π* *pi	Equivalent to about 3.14, π is an infinite non-repeating decimal, so a rounded value of π gives an inaccurate answer. Leaving the answer 'in terms of π', gives, in effect, an exact answer, e.g. Use the formula $A = \pi r^2$ to find the exact area of a circle with radius 5 cm. Answer, in terms of π: $A = \pi r^2$ $$A = \pi \times 5^2$$ $$A = \pi \times 25$$ $$A = 25\pi$$

If the question says:	The question means:
Give answer correct to 2 dp* *decimal places	Give your answer to the required degree of accuracy, e.g. 2 decimal places, 3 significant figures. You will lose marks if you do not do so.
Give answer to a sensible/ appropriate degree of accuracy	Provide an answer that is no more accurate than the degree of accuracy of the values in the question, e.g. if the lowest degree of accuracy of values given in the question is 2 significant figures, then your answer can be no more accurate than 2 significant figures. If no degree of accuracy is stated then use 3 significant figures as standard. It is always better to write down more figures as shown on your calculator before rounding your answer.
Hence	This is used in part questions and means use what you have just found in the previous part to find a solution.
Hence, or otherwise	Again for part questions, use the previous answer to proceed, but if you cannot see how to do so, you can use another method.
Make x the subject	Rearrange a formula and get x (or other letter) on one side of the equals sign and everything else (including numbers) on the other.
Measure	Use a ruler or protractor to measure a length or angle.
Not drawn accurately	Printed next to diagrams to discourage measuring.
Not to scale	Printed next to diagrams (often circles) to discourage measuring.
Prove	Provide a rigorous algebraic or geometric proof. (Similar to 'Show that'.) You are given equivalents, but must show why they are equivalent, e.g. Prove $(x+3)^2 = x^2 + 6x + 9$ $(x+3)^2 = (x+3)(x+3)$ $(x+3)^2 = x^2 + 3x + 3x + 9$ $(x+3)^2 = x^2 + 6x + 9$
Show that	Use words, numbers or algebra to show a given answer is correct, e.g. you are given a statement and must explain why it is so.
Simplify	Collect like terms or cancel a fraction, e.g. Simplify $8a + 7b - 2a + 5b$. Answer: $6a + 12b$.
Simplify fully	Collect like terms and factorise the answer or cancel terms, so an extra numerical or algebraic step is needed. For full marks, the answer must be in its simplest form, e.g. $\frac{8}{16} = \frac{4}{8} = \frac{2}{4} = \frac{1}{2}$.
Solve	Find the value(s) of x (or other letter) that makes the equation true and write out the answer, step by step (for full marks), e.g. Solve $3x + 2 = 14$ Answer: $3x = 14 - 2$ $3x = 12$ $x = \frac{12}{3}$ $x = 4$
Use a ruler and compasses	Use a ruler, a straight edge and compasses, e.g. in constructions and loci problems. Do not rub out any construction lines.
Use an algebraic method	Do not use trial and improvement. Working with algebra must be used and if correct answer is seen without an algebraic method zero marks are awarded.
Use the graph	A calculation is not necessary, read values from the graph and use them, adding lines to the graph to show how you got your answer.
Work out; Find	Usually means that a calculation is required, which you may be able to do mentally.
Write down; State	Answer is clear and does not need any working; it should be easy to identify from the question.

10 Formulae you should know

These are the formulae that you need to learn by heart for your Edexcel GCSE (9–1) Maths exam.

Area

Rectangle = $l \times w$

Parallelogram = $b \times h$

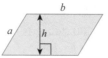

Triangle = $\frac{1}{2}b \times h$

Trapezium = $\frac{1}{2}(a \times b)h$

Circles

Circumference =
$\pi \times$ diameter, $C = \pi d$

Circumference =
$2 \times \pi \times$ radius, $C = 2\pi r$

Area of a circle =
$\pi \times$ radius squared, $A = \pi r^2$

Pythagoras

Pythagoras' theorem
For a right-angled triangle,
$a^2 + b^2 = c^2$

Trigonometric ratios (*new to F*)

$\sin x° = \dfrac{\text{opp}}{\text{hyp}}, \quad \cos x° = \dfrac{\text{adj}}{\text{hyp}},$

$\tan x° = \dfrac{\text{opp}}{\text{adj}}$

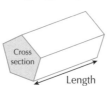

Volumes

Cuboid = $l \times w \times h$

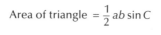

Prism = area of cross section × length

Cylinder = $\pi r^2 h$

Compound measures

Speed

$\text{speed} = \dfrac{\text{distance}}{\text{time}}$

Density

$\text{density} = \dfrac{\text{mass}}{\text{volume}}$

Pressure
The formula for pressure does not need to be learnt, and will be given within the relevant examination questions.

Higher tier formulae
Quadratic equations

The quadratic formula
The solutions of $ax^2 + bx + c = 0$,

where $a \neq 0$, are given by $x = \dfrac{-b \pm \sqrt{(b^2 - 4ac)}}{2a}$

Volumes

Volume of pyramid

$= \dfrac{1}{3} \times$ area of base $\times h$

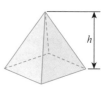

Trigonometric formulae

Sine rule $\dfrac{a}{\sin A} = \dfrac{b}{\sin B} = \dfrac{c}{\sin B}$

Cosine rule $a^2 = b^2 + c^2 - 2bc \cos A$

Area of triangle $= \dfrac{1}{2} ab \sin C$

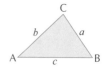

11 Further hints

Box plots: often complement the cumulative frequency (cf) curve and show the distribution of data. The two 'whiskers' represent the smallest and largest values and the box is definedby the upper quartile and the lower quartile. The median value is also represented on a box plot.

Cumulative frequency (cf): Think 'running total' when calculating the cumulative frequency column. To draw a cumulative frequency curve, plot the cumulative frequency against the end points of the class widths (*not* the midpoints!).

Circumference of a circle:

twice times *pi* times radius, or $C = 2\pi r$

Exterior angle of a regular polygon:

360 degrees divided by number of sides,
or $E = \dfrac{360°}{n}$

Factorise: extracting 'common elements', e.g.

$4x + 6 = 2(2x + 3)$
$10x^2 + 15x = 5x(2x + 3)$
$x^2 + 5x + 6 = (x + 3)(x + 2)$

You can use the 'add and multiply rule' when the coefficient of x^2 is 1. Find two numbers that **add** up to give the coefficient of x and **multiply** to give the constant term. When the coefficient of x^2 is not 1, you can use intuition or the method of factorising in pairs.

Histograms with unequal intervals: You calculate frequency density as frequency divided by class width to 'dampen down' the wide bars and 'big up' the thin bars. By representing frequency density on the vertical axis, it ensures that the areas of the bars now represent their true frequencies.

Hypotenuse squared:

opposite squared + adjacent squared

Hypothesis: a testable statement.

Interior angle of a regular polygon:

180 degrees minus the exterior angle,
or $I = 180° - E$

Laws of indices:

$A^m \times A^n = A^{m+n}$
$A^m \div A^n = A^{m-n}$

$A^{-m} = \dfrac{1}{A^m}$

$A^{\frac{m}{n}} = n\sqrt{A^m}$ (e.g. $\dfrac{8^2}{3} = \sqrt[3]{8^2} = \sqrt[3]{64} = 4$)

$A^0 = 1$
$A^1 = A$

Laws of surds:

$\sqrt{A} \times \sqrt{B} = \sqrt{AB}$
$\sqrt{A} \div \sqrt{B} = \sqrt{(A \div B)}$

To simplify a surd you need to find the highest square number factor:

$$\sqrt{8} = \sqrt{(4 \times 2)} = \sqrt{4} \times \sqrt{2} = 2\sqrt{2}$$

Median (relating to cf): is halfway up the cumulative frequency curve. The median is also called the second quartile or Q^2.

Q^1 is the lower quartile, LQ, and is one-quarter of the way up the cf curve.

Q^3 is the upper quartile, UQ, and is three-quarters of the way up the cf curve.

Values for Q^1, Q^2, and Q^3 are found by interpolation (i.e. drawing lines across to the cf curve, hit the curve and read off the values along the horizontal axis).

One linear – one quadratic simultaneous equation: Use this strategy.

i   Substitute from the linear equation into the quadratic equation. Use algebraic techniques to solve f(x) = 0.

ii Note that this often involves solving a quadratic equation.

Probability: P(E) = number of successes or number of outcomes

For independent events:
P(A and B) = P(A) × P(B)

For exclusive events:
P(A or B) = P(A) + P(B)

Tree diagrams are very helpful for representing probability situations involving more than one event.

The probability values on the branches leading off each node must add up to 1.

Simultaneous equations: Use this strategy:

i   Can I eliminate one of the variables if I add or subtract the two equations?

ii If the answer is 'no', equalise the coefficients for one of the variables by multiplying through by a number.

iii When one variable is found, substitute to find the other variable.

Sum of the angles in any polygon:

$S = 180(n - 2)$ where n = number of sides

The equation of a straight line: $y = mx + c$

m is the gradient or steepness and c is the y intercept.

If a line is sloping upwards from left to right it has a positive gradient.

If a line is sloping downwards from left to right it has a negative gradient.

If two lines are perpendicular, then the product of their gradients is –1.

The interquartile range (IQR): gives the measure of spread of 50% of the data around the average. By comparing the IQR from two samples you can see if one sample is more consistent or has greater variation compared with another sample.

Transformation geometry: You can transform a shape using a reflection, translation, rotation, enlargement or stretch. You must be as specific as possible when describing transformations.

Reflection: line of reflection must be stated.

Translation: translation vector must be given.

Rotation: centre of rotation, number of degrees and direction (clockwise or anti-clockwise) must be given.

Enlargement: centre of enlargement must be given. Remember that if the scale factor is less than one, then the enlargement is, in fact, a reduction.

Trigonometry: involves sides and angles. Work systematically through the 'formula, substitution, work out, check' strategy. Use 'SOH CAH TOA' to find the required angle or side.

Trigonometry involving non-right-angled triangles:

If you have two sides and the included angle, use the cosine rule.

If you don't have two sides and the included angle, use the sine rule.

To find an angle given three sides in a non-right angled triangle, rearrange the cosine rule.

To find the area of a triangle given two sides and included angle use:

$$A = \frac{1}{2} ab \sin C$$